Thinking Numbers

Math Games and Activities to Stimulate Creative Thinking

by
Bob Bernstein

illustrated by
Bron Smith

Cover by Bron Smith
Copyright © Good Apple, Inc., 1989
ISBN No. 0-86653-506-3
Printing No. 98765432

Good Apple, Inc.
Box 299
Carthage, IL 62321-0299

Table of Contents

GA1094

Dedicated

To Estelle, Max and Paul

GA1094

Introduction

Thinking Numbers was designed especially for the classroom teacher who is constantly on the lookout for unique and interesting ways to challenge the students' learning capacity in the area of elementary mathematics. The material presented here places a strong emphasis on defining the particular skills to be covered in each activity. All the activities may be used in a large or small group instructional setting, and many are reproducible, allowing students to work independently. Children enjoy learning through a discovery approach. *Thinking Numbers* is a discovery approach either for remediation or enrichment practice.

The activities, concepts and creative ideas presented in this book come from many enjoyable years of being in the classroom. They come because I have been fortunate enough to work with many super teachers, whose overriding goals are to reach the total child—the child who can think, listen and communicate and who can diverge thought and be creative when reaching answers.

I like to think that the child-tested ideas written in this book are the kinds of things that creative teachers will use to explore, improvise and embellish daily curriculum lessons. It is my hope that the activities presented will open wide learning vistas for children.

The pages are written primarily for you, the classroom teacher. It is hoped that you will use them to encourage exciting and ongoing discussions. In most instances the pages are left open-ended so as to have a greater impact on the creativity of you and your students.

I have tried to use as much relevant material as possible. That is why you will see activities about cars, VCR's, traffic lights and the stock market. There is also a definite attempt to cross disciplines whenever it fits a creative purpose. This can be observed in the Hall of Fame activity involving social studies and Ask Honeybee, the language arts and word problem activity.

Read through the book. Familiarize yourself with the ideas presented and then allow your own creative self to take charge. In other words, put yourself into these activities. Consider how you might be able to take a particular idea vertically, that is, how you might be able to take this idea to various grade levels. Also consider how you might now take the same activity horizontally and cross disciplines using the same format.

Combining these ideas with your own creative presentations can only lead to smiling student faces and to that tremendous personal satisfaction that only we teachers are fortunate to experience.

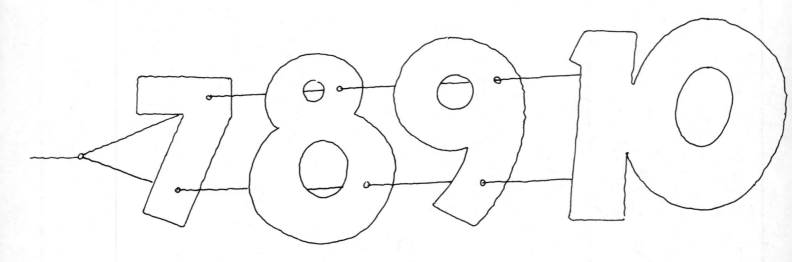

GA1094

Understanding a Million

SKILLS: Working with Large Numbers
Place Value
Multiplication, Division

Sometimes in conversations with friends and family members you might hear people say such things as, "I've seen this thing happen a million times," or "I must have heard this question asked a million times," or "There must be a million people living today in this building." Probably when people make these statements they really do not have a clear meaning as to what a million really consists of. The questions that should be asked first are probably something like:

Just what is a million all about?

What would it be like to see a million candy bars, a million hamburgers, a million people, a million dollars, or a million anything?

What is a million?

A million hamburgers? Burp!

What if you were able to save a million pennies? (Let's record this as 1,000,000 pennies.) How much money would you have?

The chart below might help you to better understand the concept of a million.

Another way to approach the concept of a million pennies is to make yourself aware of the decimal point factor. Follow the pattern of moving the decimal point two places beginning at the far right of the number and moving to the left.

Pennies	Dollar Amount
10	1 dime
100	1 dollar
1000	10 dollars
10,000	100 dollars
100,000	1000 dollars
1,000,000	10,000 dollars

Pennies		Dollar Amount
10	=	.10
100	=	1.00
1000	=	10.00
10,000	=	100.00
100,000	=	1000.00
1,000,000	=	10,000.00

GA1094

Come and get it!

For a Million, Your Cost Would Be . . .

Answer

If . . .	then	a million . . .	
a.	one candy bar costs $.75		candy bars would cost . . .	
b.	one bottle of cola costs $.90		bottles of cola would cost . . .	
c.	one plain hamburger costs $1.25		plain hamburgers would cost . . .	
d.	one cheeseburger costs $1.65		cheeseburgers would cost . . .	
e.	one sticky bun costs $1.00		sticky buns would cost . . .	
f.	one taco costs $1.49		tacos would cost . . .	
g.	one hot dog costs $1.01		hot dogs would cost . . .	
h.	one single dip cone of ice cream costs $1.05		single dip cones of ice cream would cost . . .	
i.	one plain pizza costs $7.25		plain pizzas would cost . . .	
j.	one large bag of potato chips costs $1.29		large bags of potato chips would cost . . .	

GA1094

The following is a question that you may have thought about at one time: How high is a million inches?

Again, the chart below should be helpful in your quest to discover the answer. Some of the chart is left for you to complete.

12 in.	=	1 ft.
10 ft.	=	120 in.
100 ft.	=	1200 in.
1000 ft.	=	
10,000 ft.	=	
90,000 ft.	=	

● It will be helpful for you to know that 5280 feet = 1 mile.

What if you were asked to count off seconds? How much time would elapse in 1,000,000 seconds? Set up a chart similar to the one represented above and you should be able to arrive at a fairly decent answer.

Once you arrive at an answer regarding 1,000,000 seconds, you could probably determine the number of seconds in a year!

GA1094

A Million Dollars Could Buy . . .

If you had exactly one million dollars to spend, how many of each of the following items would your million dollars buy?

	Item	Cost	
1.	automobile	$20,000	_____ automobiles
2.	boat	$40,000	_____ boats
3.	house	$125,000	_____ houses
4.	ranch	$500,000	_____ ranches
5.	airplane	$310,000	_____ airplanes
6.	horse	$50,000	_____ horses
7.	skateboard	$100	_____ skateboards
8.	video cassette recorder	$350	_____ VCRs
9.	video cam-corder	$1000	_____ video cam-corders
10.	give to charities	$35,000 to each charity	_____ charities

Now that you have been thinking of one million, you might want to consider one billion.

My other boat is a yacht!

S.S. DINGHY

4

Split Second Addition

SKILLS: Basic Addition Facts
             Patterning
             Subtraction

Follow the directions and you will be able to add a column of five addends in a split second (notice the adjective *split*). You will be able to determine the sum in any of the problems presented to you.

A	B	C	D	E
432	146	523	367	59
36	344	226	565	455
135	47	424	169	257
333	443	127	466	158
234	245	325	268	356

figure A

1. Have someone record on paper (or the chalkboard) five addends from the chart above. Addends must be chosen, one from each column, headed by the letters A, B, C, D and E.

Example: 432
                  344
                  424
                  268
                   59

*Instead of one student recording addends, it might be more interesting if five, ten or even the entire class chooses their own problems.

     GA1094

2. Once the students have set up their addition problems, inform them that you will be able to tell each of them the sum of their own problem even though you will not see their work. Tell them that you will have their answer in a split second.

3. Instruct the participants that all you want to know about their individual problem is *the sum total of all the units in the one's column.* As soon as you are aware of this total you will be able to give the answer to the entire problem again without ever seeing their choices of addends.

4. In the example given, the student should tell you that the sum of the one's column is 27. Sometimes a student might say that he has 7 in the one's column, but this is not what you asked for. You want the total in the one's column, and in this instance the correct answer is 27. Once you hear that the one's column totals 27, you may now respond with the sum of the problem as 1527.

Try to discover the solution by searching for a pattern.

Student response to one's column	Your part of the answer	Your answer to the total problem
24	18	1824
16	26	2616
12	30	3012
22	20	2022
38	4	438

The solution can be found on the next page.

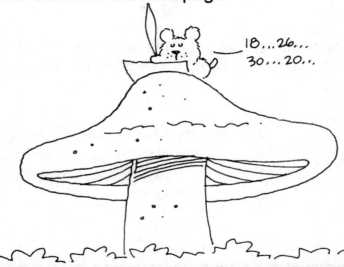

18...26...
30...20...

The solution, answer and secret is to take the sum of the one's column and find the difference from 42. In the example, the one's column totaled 27 and the difference from 42 is 15. Therefore the answer to the problem is 1527.

Again, if the one's column totaled 22, the difference from 42 is 20. Therefore the answer is 2022. This works every time with the addends in figure A.

For additional patterns, check figure A again.

1. Notice the digit in the ten's column.
2. Notice the sum of the digits in the hundred's column and the one's column.

Check column C.

Ten's digits are all 2's.

Hundred's digit and one's digit all total 8.

By being aware of these patterns, you should be able to create your own additional addends for each column.

You know what digit must be in the ten's column. You also know what the sum of the hundred's and one's digit must be.

Below is another table (figure B). The rules for operation are basically the same, but this time the secret operating number is not 42. This figure works well with 101.

F	G	H	I	J
911	454	834	148	625
218	850	339	445	724
614	256	636	49	328
317	58	735	247	229
515	157	537	643	526

figure B

Additional patterns . . .

Refer to column J. Look at differences such as . . .

724	625	328
−625	−526	−229
99	99	99

Does this hold true for all of the columns?

7

Split Second
Addition Fill-Ins

K	L	M	N	O
245	6	6	6	3
6	327	8	2	6
3	1	415	1	8
2	2	4	533	5
6	5	7	5	903

P	Q	R	S	T
4	7	1	3	314
3	5	0	436	2
2	4	244	5	6
7	820	3	1	5
504	5	1	2	7

GA1094

Good Morning

SKILLS: Computational Skills
Renaming Numbers

Good morning.

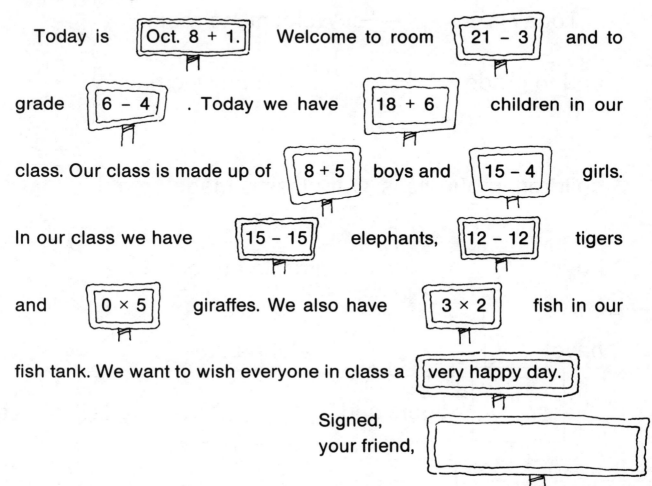

Today is [Oct. 8 + 1.] Welcome to room [21 – 3] and to grade [6 – 4] . Today we have [18 + 6] children in our class. Our class is made up of [8 + 5] boys and [15 – 4] girls.

In our class we have [15 – 15] elephants, [12 – 12] tigers and [0 × 5] giraffes. We also have [3 × 2] fish in our fish tank. We want to wish everyone in class a [very happy day.]

Signed,
your friend, [   ]

The following is an open-ended and creative way to begin all of your school days. The story format presented on the next page can be replicated into a somewhat larger display. It can be permanently taped to the chalkboard with the equations of that particular day erased at the end of the school day so that the story format will be ready for your children's creative responses the next day.

For example, on October 10, a student might do something such as . . .

Today is [Oct. 2 + 2 + 2 + 2 + 2.] Welcome to room [17 + 1] and to grade [11 – 9,] etc.

This activity will help you encourage creativity on the part of your students.

GA1094

Good morning,

Today is _____ . Welcome to room _____

and to grade _____ . Today we have _____

children in our class. Our class is made up of _____

boys and _____ girls. In our class we _____

have _____ elephants,

tigers and _____ giraffes. We

also have _____ fish in our fish tank. We want

to wish everyone in class a _____ .

Signed,
your friend, _____

10

GA1094

Patchwork Quilt

SKILLS: Coordinates   Basic Primary Skills
        Inequalities   Place Value
        Base Two

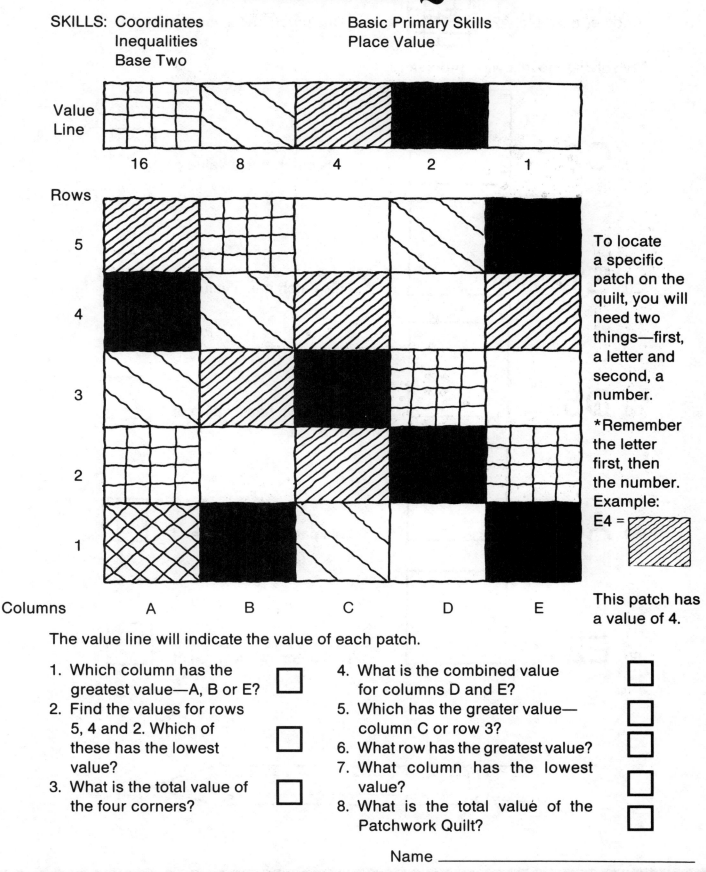

To locate a specific patch on the quilt, you will need two things—first, a letter and second, a number.

*Remember the letter first, then the number.
Example:
E4 =

This patch has a value of 4.

The value line will indicate the value of each patch.

1. Which column has the greatest value—A, B or E?

2. Find the values for rows 5, 4 and 2. Which of these has the lowest value?

3. What is the total value of the four corners?

4. What is the combined value for columns D and E?

5. Which has the greater value—column C or row 3?

6. What row has the greatest value?

7. What column has the lowest value?

8. What is the total value of the Patchwork Quilt?

Name _____

GA1094

Another example: A2 = This patch has a value of 16.

Try solving the following problems:

10. **C2** =   This patch has a value of   .

20. **E1** =   This patch has a value of   .

30. **D5** =   This patch has a value of   .

40. **A5** =   This patch has a value of   .

50. **E2** =   This patch has a value of   .

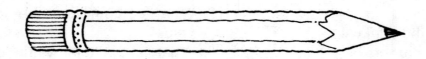

GA1094

Name _____

Patch These Quilts

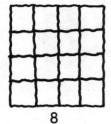 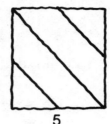 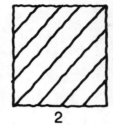  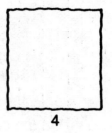

8   5   2   7   4

a. 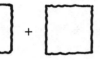 + □ + ▦ = _____   i.   = _____

b. + ■ + ▦ = _____   j. = _____

c. [] □ = _____   k.   = _____

d. [ ] □ = _____   l. [ ] ÷ = _____

e. [] ■ = _____   m. [] = _____

f. [] = _____   n.   = _____

g. [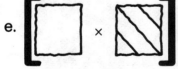] = _____   o.  = _____

h.  = _____   p. [ ] 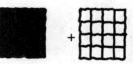 = _____

 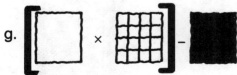 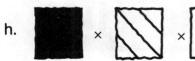   

13

It's All in Black and White

SKILLS: Patterning   Prime Numbers
        Factors   Palindromes
        Square Numbers   Money

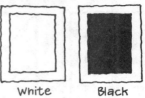

White   Black

The columns listed on the next few pages are lettered A through L. Each column, A through K, contains its own pattern.

   Example:
     Suppose a column had the following numbers:
        90, 10, 70, 60, 20.
The pattern answer is multiples of 10.

Discover and record your answers to the number patterns that follow.

*Column L is for you to create your own pattern.

A		B		C		D
29		42		3		9
24		18		10		81
21		4		1		64
26		22		30		25
23		6		5		36
25		16		6		100

GA1094

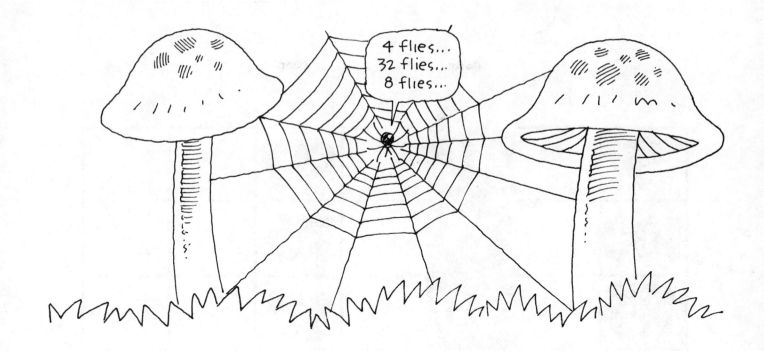

E		F		G		H
23				**4**		707
11		366		**32**		1331
5		60		**8**		232
17		7		**64**		88
2		365		**2**		121
19		24		**16**		515

15

I		J		K		L
5		45		97		
100		15		76		
25		90		17		
10		105		87		
50		75		73		
1		30		57		

I   J   K   L

A _____   G _____

B _____   H _____

C _____   I _____

D _____   J _____

E _____   K _____

F _____   L _____

16

Hundred Board Discoveries

SKILLS: Patterning
        Addition Facts

This exercise involves the use of squares on a hundred board. As you get into this activity you will see some very interesting patterns emerge. The following number chart is to be considered for this activity.

figure A

1	2	3	4	5	6
7	8	9	10	11	12
13	14	15	16	17	18
19	20	21	22	23	24
25	26	27	28	29	30
31	32	33	34	35	36

Let's begin our discovery search with a 3 × 3 section of the number chart.

1	2	3
7	8	9
13	14	15

    GA1094

The middle number in the grid is 8. A discovery is that 3 times the middle number should be equal to the sum of either diagonal line or the middle vertical line. In this instance, each line in this grid should total 24 . . . 3 × the middle number = 24   3 × 8 = 24

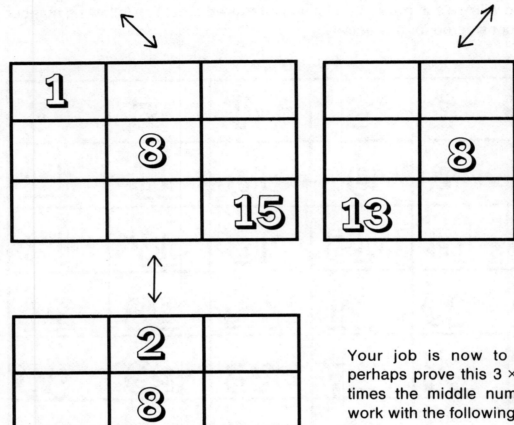

Your job is now to check and perhaps prove this 3 × 3 theory (3 times the middle number). Will it work with the following grids?

I think I made a new discovery!

GA1094

13	14	15
19	20	21
25	26	27

22	23	24
28	29	30
34	35	36

Let us now extend our pattern search to 4 × 4 grids. Again our reference point will be figure A.

1	2	3	4
7	8	9	10
13	14	15	16
19	20	21	22

The sum of the inside square (8 + 9 + 14 + 15) is 46. It would therefore seem proper if all discoveries involving the above grid were to total 46.

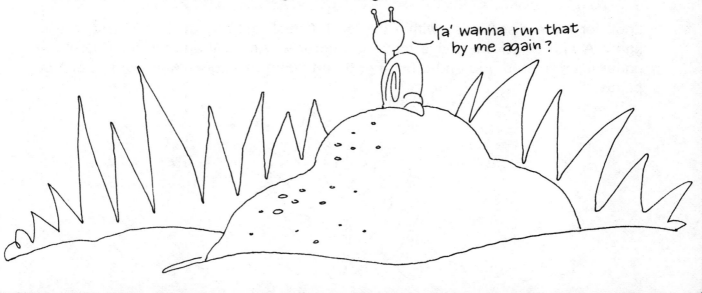

"Ya' wanna run that by me again?"

GA1094

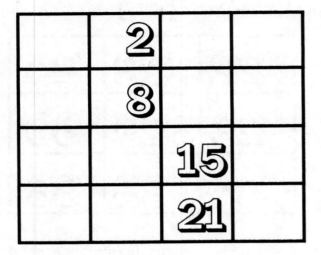

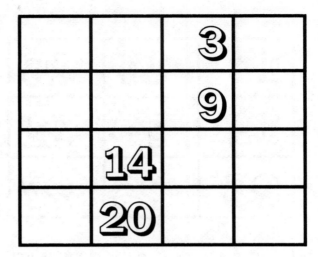

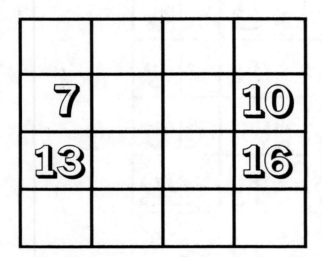

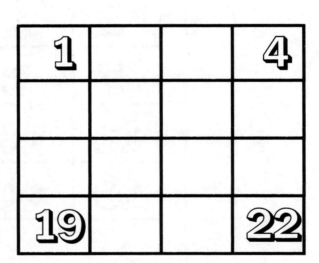

Look for more discoveries within this grid. Check out any other 4 × 4 square in figure A and see if the above patterns hold true. And still another idea. Look for patterns on a 5 × 5 grid and a 6 × 6 grid and again use figure A as your reference point.

Boy! that looks like FUN!

GA1094

Who's Who, Past and Present

SKILLS: Basic Computational Skills
         Base Two
         Place Value

No, you don't look like Abraham Lincoln to me!

Have someone look at the Hall of Fame chart and make a selection of one of the fifty names on the list. The student making the selection is not to tell you his choice. Once the student has made a choice, he should now refer to the chart headed by the letters A, B, C, D, E and F. (The names in this chart are alphabetized according to last name.) The student is to tell you the column or columns in which his choice appears.

For example:

Suppose the student's choice is Harry Truman. What he must tell you is not the name of his choice but the column or columns in which the name appears. "My selection appears in columns A, C and D."

To learn the name that was chosen, all you have to do is give a numerical value to each column heading as indicated

A	B	C	D	E	F
32	16	8	4	2	1

In the example above, the columns mentioned were A, C and D. If you use the values assigned to these columns, you would arrive at the following:

A		C		D	
32	+	8	+	4	= 44

Refer to the Hall of Fame chart and you will see that 44 is assigned to Harry Truman.

Hall of Fame

1. John Adams
2. Marian Anderson
3. Joan of Arc
4. Neil Armstrong
5. John Barrymore
6. Jim Bowie
7. Julius Caesar
8. Jimmy Carter
9. Winston Churchill
10. Davy Crockett
11. George A. Custer
12. Sandra Day O'Connor
13. Jefferson Davis
14. Frederick Douglass
15. Amelia Earhart
16. Dwight Eisenhower
17. Queen Elizabeth
18. Ben Franklin
19. Robert Frost
20. John Glenn
21. Mikhail Gorbachev
22. U.S. Grant
23. Nathaniel Hawthorne
24. Ernest Hemingway
25. Patrick Henry
26. Lyndon Johnson
27. John Paul Jones
28. John F. Kennedy
29. Martin Luther King
30. Robert E. Lee.
31. Abraham Lincoln
32. Douglas MacArthur
33. James Madison
34. Florence Nightingale
35. Richard Nixon
36. William Penn
37. Molly Pitcher
38. Edgar A. Poe
39. Ronald Reagan
40. Sally Ride
41. Franklin D. Roosevelt
42. Alan Shepard
43. Gilbert Sullivan
44. Harry Truman
45. Harriet Tubman
46. Queen Victoria
47. Earl Warren
48. George Washington
49. Martha Washington
50. Woodrow Wilson

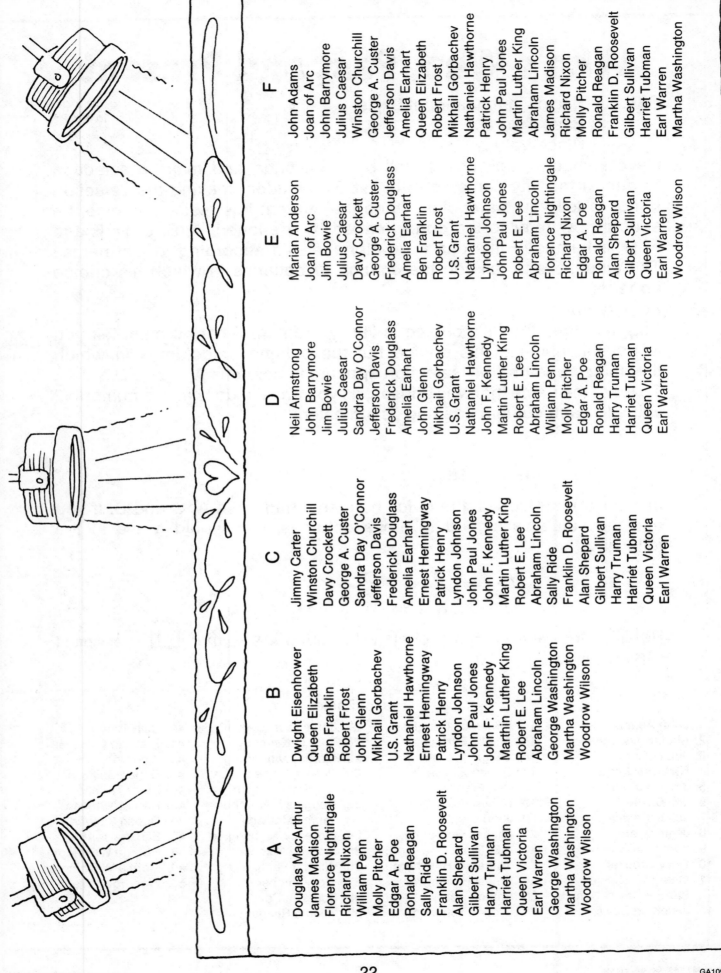

A	B	C	D	E	F
Douglas MacArthur	Dwight Eisenhower	Jimmy Carter	Neil Armstrong	Marian Anderson	John Adams
James Madison	Queen Elizabeth	Winston Churchill	John Barrymore	Joan of Arc	Joan of Arc
Florence Nightingale	Ben Franklin	Davy Crockett	Jim Bowie	Jim Bowie	John Barrymore
Richard Nixon	Robert Frost	George A. Custer	Julius Caesar	Julius Caesar	Julius Caesar
William Penn	John Glenn	Sandra Day O'Connor	Sandra Day O'Connor	Davy Crockett	Winston Churchill
Molly Pitcher	Mikhail Gorbachev	Jefferson Davis	Jefferson Davis	George A. Custer	George A. Custer
Edgar A. Poe	U.S. Grant	Frederick Douglass	Frederick Douglass	Frederick Douglass	Jefferson Davis
Ronald Reagan	Nathaniel Hawthorne	Amelia Earhart	Amelia Earhart	Amelia Earhart	Amelia Earhart
Sally Ride	Ernest Hemingway	Ernest Hemingway	John Glenn	Ben Franklin	Queen Elizabeth
Franklin D. Roosevelt	Patrick Henry	Patrick Henry	Mikhail Gorbachev	Robert Frost	Robert Frost
Alan Shepard	Lyndon Johnson	Lyndon Johnson	U.S. Grant	U.S. Grant	Mikhail Gorbachev
Gilbert Sullivan	John Paul Jones	John Paul Jones	Nathaniel Hawthorne	Nathaniel Hawthorne	Nathaniel Hawthorne
Harry Truman	John F. Kennedy	John F. Kennedy	John F. Kennedy	Lyndon Johnson	Patrick Henry
Harriet Tubman	Martin Luther King	Martin Luther King	Martin Luther King	John Paul Jones	John Paul Jones
Queen Victoria	Robert E. Lee	Robert E. Lee	Robert E. Lee	Robert E. Lee	Martin Luther King
Earl Warren	Abraham Lincoln	Abraham Lincoln	Abraham Lincoln	Abraham Lincoln	Abraham Lincoln
George Washington	George Washington	Sally Ride	William Penn	Florence Nightingale	James Madison
Martha Washington	Martha Washington	Franklin D. Roosevelt	Molly Pitcher	Richard Nixon	Richard Nixon
Woodrow Wilson	Woodrow Wilson	Alan Shepard	Edgar A. Poe	Edgar A. Poe	Molly Pitcher
		Gilbert Sullivan	Ronald Reagan	Ronald Reagan	Ronald Reagan
		Harry Truman	Harry Truman	Alan Shepard	Franklin D. Roosevelt
		Harriet Tubman	Harriet Tubman	Gilbert Sullivan	Gilbert Sullivan
		Queen Victoria	Queen Victoria	Queen Victoria	Harriet Tubman
		Earl Warren	Earl Warren	Earl Warren	Earl Warren
				Woodrow Wilson	Martha Washington

GA1094

Name _____

Use the Hall of Fame list to complete the numerical value distribution of the following:

	32	16	8	4	2	1	
Example: Jim Bowie				X	X		= 6
Winston Churchill							=
Davy Crockett							=
Queen Elizabeth							=
Ben Franklin							=
John Glenn							=
U.S. Grant							=
Ernest Hemingway							=
Patrick Henry							=
John F. Kennedy							=
Robert E. Lee							=
William Penn							=
Sally Ride							=
Harriet Tubman							=

(Hall of Fame values: Winston Churchill = 9, Davy Crockett = 10, Queen Elizabeth = 17, Ben Franklin = 18, John Glenn = 20, U.S. Grant = 22, Ernest Hemingway = 24, Patrick Henry = 25, John F. Kennedy = 28, Robert E. Lee = 30, William Penn = 36, Sally Ride = 40, Harriet Tubman = 45)

Ask Honeybee!

SKILL: Word Problems

Can you solve these problems?

Dear Honeybee,

I am 12 years old and I am very much in love with an older woman who is 1½ times my age. Should I ask her to go steady or will she be too old for me when I reach 30?

Macho Mike

Dear Bee,

John wants to buy T-shirts for his friends. He has twice as many friends as I. I have three times the number of pals as Mary. I know she has four friends. How many T-shirts must John buy?

Signed,
Looking Out

P.S. If the shirts cost $3.89 each, how much money will John need?

Dear Honey,

Susie wants a new TV. She says it will cost $280. Her sister Lisa will give her half of what she needs. Her best friend Vicki will give her one quarter of the cost of the TV. How much money will Susie still need to buy the 13-inch remote?

Signed,
Tall Paul

P.S. Susie has $33.08. I know this is not enough. How much more money does she need?

In the classroom, set up a bulletin board area or a learning station and encourage the class to solve problems written to Honeybee. Encourage students to create their own letters.

24

GA1094

Fraction Action

SKILLS: Addition of Fractions
        Equivalent Fractions

This is a game for two to four players. The game is played with rules similar to that of an old children's game, a card game called war. In this game the cards were shuffled and then dealt evenly among the players. The players were to keep their cards facedown, and when it was their turn they were to expose the top card from their facedown pile, and the player with the card showing the greatest value was declared to be the winner of that round. The play continued until all of the cards were shown. At the end of a designated time period, the winner was the player with the most cards. Fraction Action has rules similar to those described above.

Follow this round of play between players A, B and C.

A		B		C	
3/8	1/4	3/8	3/8	1/8	1/8
1/8	1/8	1/4	1/8	1/8	1/4

If you total their cards, A = $^7/_8$, B = $^9/_8$ = $1^1/_8$, C = $^5/_8$. Player B is the winner of the round and would collect the lesser cards from A and C. B would add these two cards to his pile of unused cards. The three players would then begin to play the next round.

GA1094

Fraction Action

Playing cards for Fraction Action

1	1/8	1	1/4
1/8	1/8	1/8	1/8

1/2	1/2	1/8	1/4	3/8	3/8	1/4	1/8
1/2	1/8	1/8	1/4	3/8	1/8	1/4	1

1/4	1/4	1/4	1/4	1	1/4	1/8	1/8
1/4	1/8	1/8	3/8	1/8	1/8	1/8	1/8

1/8	3/8	1/8	1/4	1/8	3/8	1/8	1/8
5/8	1/4	1/2	1	3/8	1/8	1/4	1/4

GA1094

Fraction Action

Playing cards for Fraction Action

1/2	1/8	1/4	1/4	1	1/2	1/4	1
1/8	1/8	1/4	1/4	1/4	1/4	1/4	1/4

1/2	1/2	1/2	1/8	1/8	1/2	1	1/8
1/2	1/2	1/8	1/2	1/8	1/8	1/8	1/8

3/8	1/8	3/8	3/8	1/8	5/8	1/8	1/4
1/8	1/2	3/8	1/8	1/8	1/8	3/8	3/8

1/4	1/4	1	1/4
1/4	3/8	1/4	1/4

Fraction Action can be made somewhat easier to play. This can be accomplished by cutting the playing cards in half and thereby having twice as many cards.

With the playing cards cut in half, the equivalences that students must know are easier.

1/8	3/8
1/4	1/4

1/8	3/8
1/4	1/4

27

GA1094

Total these Fraction Action cards.

Example:

1/8	1/2
1/8	1/8

= 7/8

3/8	3/8
3/8	1/8

d. =_____

1/4	1/4
1/4	1/4

h. =_____

1/2	1/8
1/8	1/2

a. =_____

1/4	1/4
1/4	3/8

e. =_____

1/2	1/8
1/8	1/8

i. =_____

1/2	1/2
1/2	1/2

b. =_____

1	1/4
1/4	1/4

f. =_____

1/4	1
1/4	1/4

j. =_____

1	1/8
1/8	1/8

c. =_____

3/8	1/8
1/8	1/2

g. =_____

1	1/2
1/4	1/4

k. =_____

28

And the Answer Is . . .

SKILLS: Addition with Three and Four-Place Addends
Place Value
Addition with and Without Regrouping

If the answer is 604, use the addends found in a, b and c. You will then have to arrange the numerals within each addend so that the sum of all three addends in each column will equal 604.

Example:

a. 402
b. 319
c. 702

The rearrangement should be:

a.	2	0	4
b.	1	9	3
c.	2	0	7
	6	0	4

Another example:

a. 851
b. 290
c. 323

And the answer is 699.

The rearrangement:

1	5	8
2	0	9
3	3	2
6	9	9

One more example:

a. 415
b. 378
c. 210

And the answer is 652.

The rearrangement:

1	4	5
3	8	7
1	2	0
6	5	2

GA1094

And the Answer Is . . .

Solve the following problems:

1. a. 123
    b. 922
    c. 402

2	1	
	9	2
4		0
9	2	5

4. a. 117
    b. 402
    c. 300

1	7	
	0	4
3	0	
6	7	5

2. a. 219
    b. 327
    c. 284

1	9	
	3	7
4		2
9	1	1

5. a. 202
    b. 115
    c. 314

	2	0
1	5	
		3
7	8	4

3. a. 314
    b. 250
    c. 132

	3	1
	0	5
3	1	
9	4	8

6. a. 401
    b. 223
    c. 160

1		
	2	
		6
5	6	8

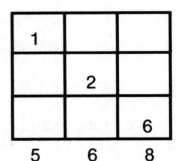

GA1094

More of And the Answer Is . . .

7. a. 2480
    b. 7113
    c. 1002

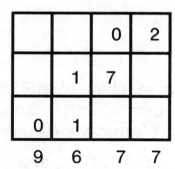

8. a. 3140
    b. 2516
    c. 4102

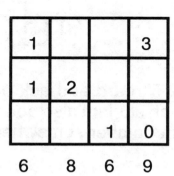

9. a. 2306
    b. 4110
    c. 3821

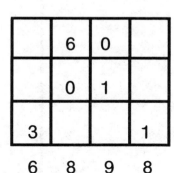

10. a. 1155
    b. 2354
    c. 2100

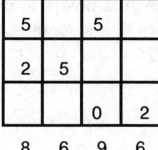

11. a. 4163
    b. 2501
    c. 3112

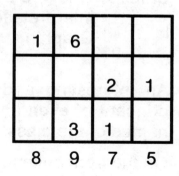

12. a. 7130
    b. 2231
    c. 4601

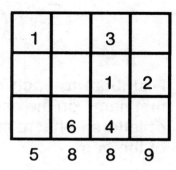

13. a. 1313
    b. 4312
    c. 1502

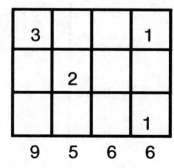

14. a. 2571
    b. 2103
    c. 2144

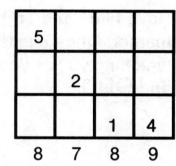

GA1094

First Name Basis

SKILLS: Odd and Even Numbers
Interpretation of Data
Graphing

An interesting and relevant idea for teaching understanding of the concept of even and odd can be accomplished by the use of the first names of the class members (and don't forget the teacher's first name).

On the front bulletin board or chalkboard, tape large and colorful cutouts of the following:

even   **odd**

Distribute to each child a white 3" x 5" card and ask him to print his first name on the card. Be sure that each student also counts the number of letters in his name and records that number somewhere on the front of the card.

Brenda

6

Have him write on his card with his favorite colors in crayon or magic marker. Once this is completed, be sure that students are listening and watching you as you write the following numbers over the words EVEN and ODD.

GA1094

even 0 2 4 6 8 10   **odd** 1 3 5 7 9 11

Tell the students that you will now call out a number and that those students who wrote their first name and also the number as to how many letters are in that name should come to the front of the room. At this point, you will give each student a piece of masking tape and ask him to tape his card in the proper column.

So that you might begin this activity in a light and nonthreatening manner, start calling the numbers . . . zero first:

> "Now that everyone has written his first name in his favorite colors and also written the number that will tell us how many letters are in his first name, . . . how many of you have a name with no letters or zero letters?" The response should be laughter!

Do the same for the numbers 1, 2 and so on. Be sure that you tape your card in the appropriate column.

The completed chart should remain on the board so that children can assimilate the even and odd concept. A follow-up activity is to turn this chart into an interesting bar graph or pictograph.

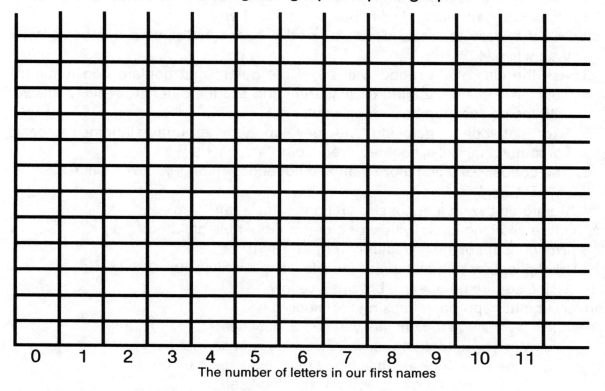

0   1   2   3   4   5   6   7   8   9   10   11
The number of letters in our first names

Can you find the number that is most popular?

33

Mickey Moose

SKILLS: Basic Computational Skills—Addition, Subtraction, Multiplication, Division
Patterning

The number moose on the next page is designed to encourage creative drill at various grade levels. The number moose will encourage creativity in the instructor as well as the students. Duplicate this moose so that it will be as large as you wish. Color in the number areas as suggested. It will create an eye-catching motivational math aid. It is also suggested that you cover the moose with clear Con-Tact paper and then tape numerals onto the color areas. This will allow you to change numerals from time to time.

The activities that can be used with the classroom aid will range from very simple to somewhat difficult depending upon the grade level of your students.

Very simple:
1. The teacher refers to the moose and calls out a color. The teacher asks the children to respond with the correct number.
2. Ask the class to respond with all of the colors that have a number greater than white (4).
3. Ask the class to respond with all of the colors that contain odd numbers.
4. Touch a piece of clothing on a student and ask the other students to answer with the correct number.   tan sweater = 2
5. Excellent tool to help students develop a better understanding of basic computational skills, such as   red + purple $1 + 9 =$
6. The concept of using more than two addends: pink + yellow + white
$5 + 3 + 4 =$
7. Reinforce the concept of subtraction: blue – tan $8 - 2 =$

Much more challenging activities for older or more able children:
8. The concept of multiplication: purple × tan $9 \times 2 =$
9. Multiplication with addition: (purple × tan) + white $(9 \times 2) + 4 =$
10. Using square numbers: brown² – yellow $10^2 - 3 =$

And still another approach to using the moose:
Teacher, "When you look at tan, you see 2, but I see 7.
When you look at yellow, you see 3, but I see 10.
When you look at white, you see 4, but I see 13.
The question now is, 'Who sees what I see?'
If you see what I see, choose a color and give me the answer."

GA1094

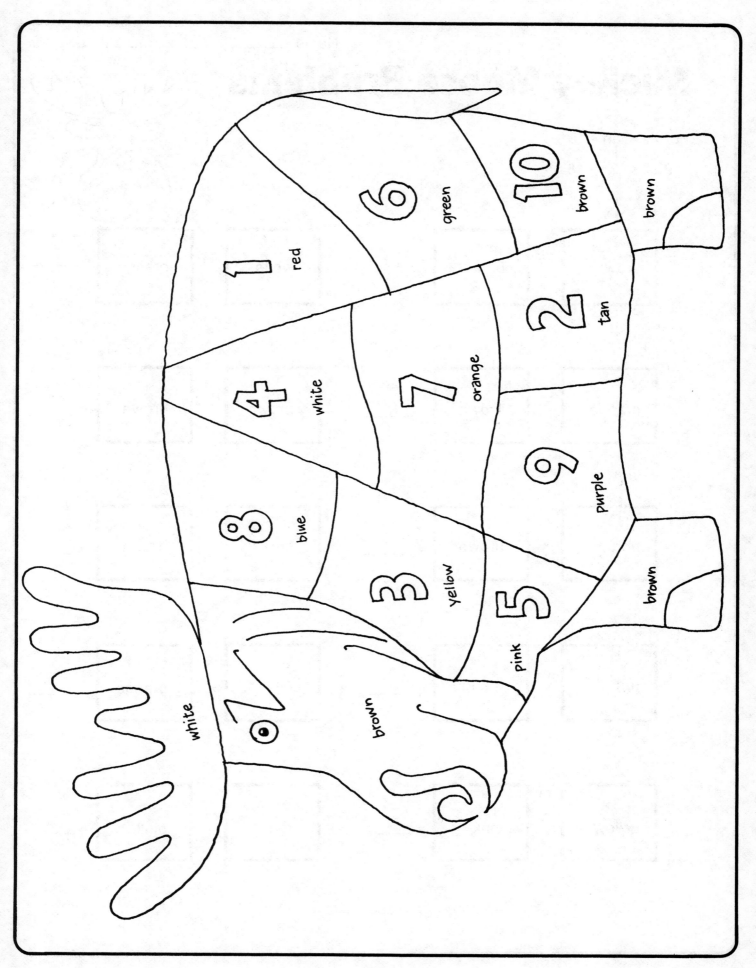

1 red
6 green
10 brown
brown
4 white
7 orange
2 tan
8 blue
3 yellow
9 purple
5 pink
brown
white
brown

35

Mickey Moose Problems

purple × tan = 18
  ↓   ↓
  9   ×   2   = 18

a. | brown | × | blue | = _____

b. | orange | × | brown | = _____

c. | purple | × | brown | = _____

d. | red | × | orange | = _____

e. | yellow | × | pink | = _____

f. | white | × | orange | = _____

g. | brown | × | brown | = _____

h. | tan | × | brown | = _____

i. | blue | × | orange | = _____

j. | red | × | pink | = _____

GA1094

With Mickey Moose as a reference point, complete the value for each color listed in the table.

Mickey Moose Tables

Example:

blue	16
brown	20
green	12
purple	18
yellow	6
white	8

tan	10
white	20
brown	50
pink	
green	
red	

a.

pink	55
brown	110
purple	99
white	
green	
pink	

c.

Answer:
2 times the original value.

blue = 8
2 × 8 = 16

brown = 10
2 × 10 = 20

green	24
purple	36
pink	20
brown	
white	
red	

b.

purple	63
green	42
white	28
yellow	
orange	
brown	

d.

37

GA1094

Finding Area

Have you seen my area?

SKILLS: Working with Area
Units of Measure
Fractions
Estimation

An interesting way to measure something is to work with various sizes of units. In dealing with area, this shape ⬜ is equal to 1 unit.

Therefore, this shape ▭ is equal to 2 units.

With these unit figures as your measuring reference point, can you find the area of these shapes?

a. _____ units

b. _____ units

c. _____ units

d. _____units

With the same shape [figure] representing a unit equal to 1, how would

Have you seen my area?

you draw figures with an area of e. 2½ units, f. 1¾ units, g. 4¼ units, h. ¼ unit?

The size of any unit can be subject to change. Suppose we now call

[figure] as the unit size equal to 1.

It would seem appropriate that [figure] is equal to an area of 1 $\frac{2}{3}$. Can you find the area of these figures?

i. _____ units   j.

_____ units

_____ units

k.

l. _____ units

GA1094

How would you draw figures with an area of m. 2 $\frac{1}{3}$ units, n. 5 units, o. 3 $\frac{2}{3}$, p. $\frac{2}{3}$ units?

Suppose we now declare 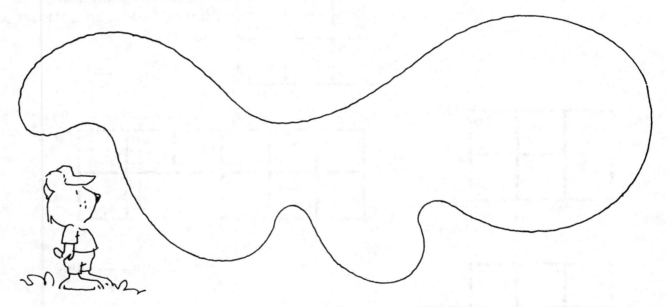 will be our unit size equal to 1,

how would you find the area of

The area of this odd shape is _____ units.

Using the same unit size (above), can you find the area of your desk, hand, foot, body?

Name _____

GA1094

Finding Area Units

This shape is equal to 1 unit.

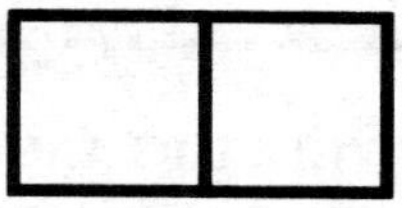

Find the value of the following:

a. 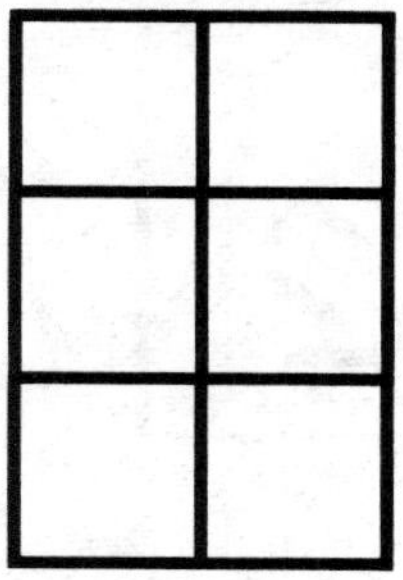 _____ units

d. 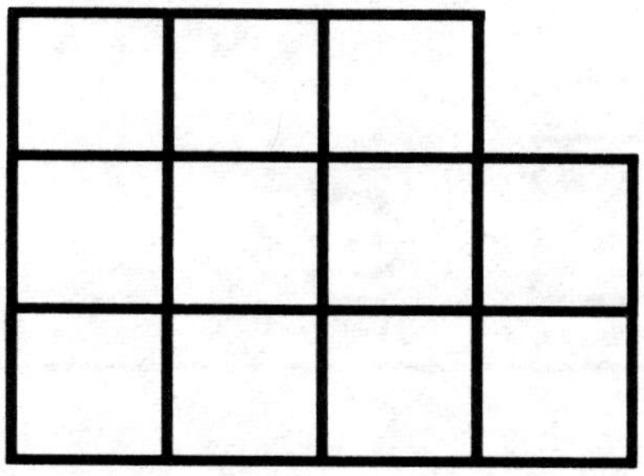 _____ units

b. 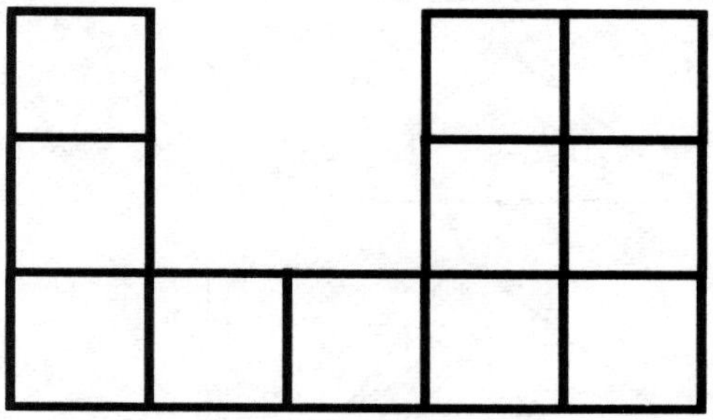 _____ units

e. 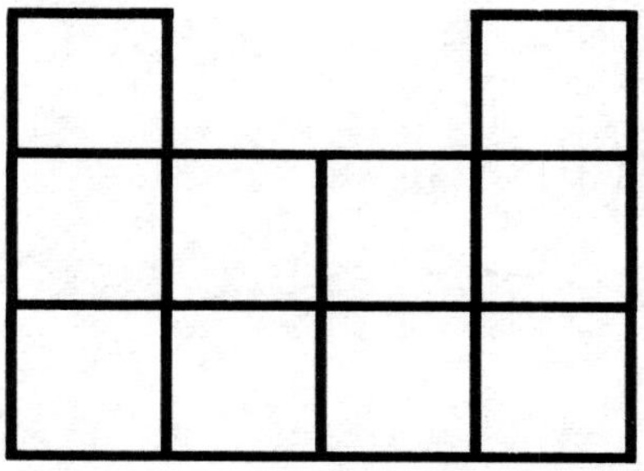 _____ units

c. 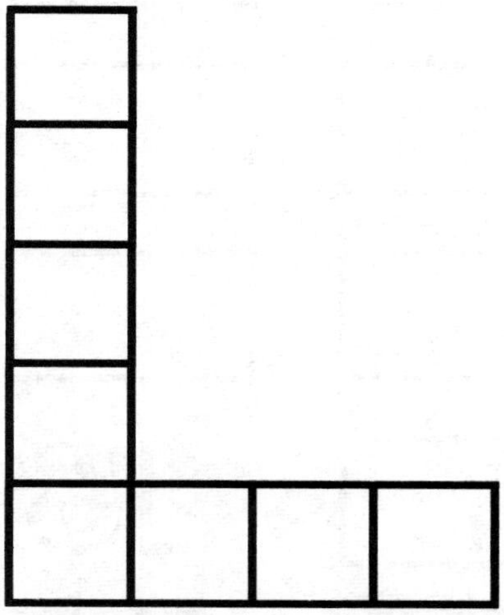 _____ units

f. 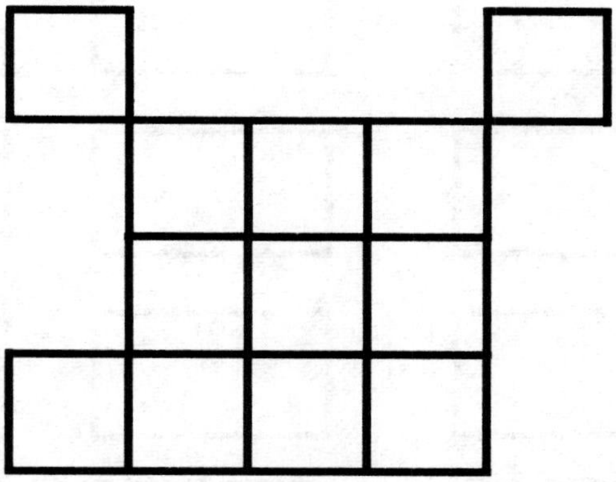 _____ units

41

Geo-Code

SKILLS: Basic Skills Facts
             Regrouping Column Addition

When you are working with the Geo-Code, the mystery begins. Add and find the correct sums.

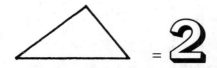

$\square$ = **5**   △ = **2**

The following are sample problems:

15   **20**   **22**   **26**   **30**

42

Can you solve this?

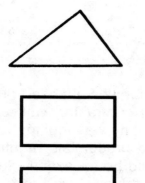

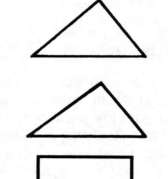

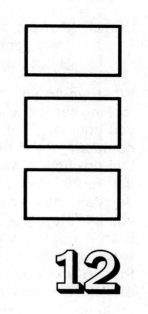

a. _____   b. _____   c. _____

This is a super problem.

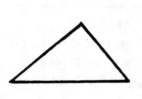

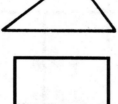

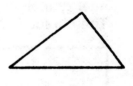

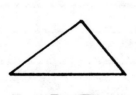

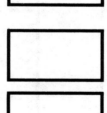

d. _____   e. _____   f. _____

Create some problems of your own.

Brainteaser V

My brain doesn't need teasing.

SKILLS: Powers of 2
Divergent Thought
Basic Addition Facts

What would you do if the following opportunity came along? Suppose you were looking for work in the construction area and a building contractor walked up to you and said that you were just the person that his company was looking for. The company noted that you had all of the proper skills and credentials required for this position. It was also noted that this job opening would be for exactly 28 days, that is 28 consecutive days with no days off. The only thing left for you now to decide is how you wish to be compensated for this four-week work period. Would you like plan A or plan B?

Plan A will pay you at the rate of $25,000 for seven days of intensive and difficult work. By the end of the 28th day you will receive a total of $100,000.

Plan B will compensate you with one penny after the first day's intensive and exhausting work and will then proceed to double your pay each and every day up to and including the 28th day.

Once again, please understand that after one week of intensive labor plan A will reward you with $25,000, and after two weeks of this back-breaking work you will receive another $25,000 for a two-week total of $50,000. Plan B will reward you with .64 cents after one week of intensive labor and a wonderful sum of $81.92 after completing two full weeks of this most difficult work.

The choice is now up to you, plan A or plan B?

PLAN A $25,000 a week 40 weeks of work (28 days)		PLAN B 1 penny after the first day, to be doubled every day up to and including the 28th day
1st week _____		1st day _____
2nd week_____		2nd day _____
3rd week _____		3rd day_____
4th week _____		4th day_____
		5th day _____
		28th day_____

Brainteaser VI

SKILL: Divergent Thought

You are given 9 cubes that look to be exact in appearance. One of the cubes, however, is a counterfeit in that this particular cube weighs somewhat less than the other 8 cubes. Looking at the cubes, you cannot tell which is the imposter.

Your job is to find the culprit. The only instrument you will have to help you locate the inferior cube is a pan balance.

When you place an equal number of cubes in each pan, the cube with the least weight will cause the pan holding it to tilt downward, thereby indicating that one of the cubes in this pan is a counterfeit. The question for you to consider is . . . What is the least number of weighings that you must make before you can safely determine which of the 9 cubes is the bogus one?

Brainteaser VII

SKILLS: Basic Computational Skills
Base Two
Divergent Thought

If you had a strip of wood 16 inches in length, could you break off pieces or better yet, could you cut off parts of the strip so that you would be able to count consecutively from 1 to 15?

For example:
Figure A represents a strip of wood that is 15 inches in length. If you cut each part exactly 1 inch long, you will then have 14 cuts made.

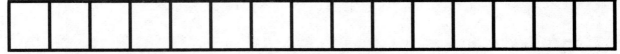

figure A

At this point, since all of the parts would be equal, you can assign a value of 1 to each part (14 cuts, but 15 parts) and then begin the count starting at one and ending at fifteen.

We know that this can easily be accomplished.

The question is can you accomplish the same feat with a strip of wood (or paper, or anything easily sliced) 15 inches in length *in a lesser number of cuts*?

GA1094

Brainteaser VIII

Anything in there to tease?

SKILL: Divergent Thought

The following number series consisting of 0 through 12 is arranged in a very unique format. Concentrate on the order as listed below and see if you are able to determine a reason for this most unusual but also most interesting pattern.

a. 8

b. 11

c. 5

d. 4

e. 9

f. 1

g. 7

h. 6

i. 10

j. 3

k. 12

l. 2

m. 0

Another view:

8, 11, 5, 4, 9, 1, 7, 6, 10, 3, 12, 2, 0

GA1094

Brainteaser IX

It's the year of the roaring twenties . . . **1928**

Can you write equations that will give you answers from **1** to **20**?
One specific rule states that in each equation you must use the digits

in **1928**. You may use any operation or combination of operations
to help you arrive at your answers.

	= 1	= 11
	= 2 [(8 ÷ 2) − 1] + 9	= 12
(2 + 1) × (9 − 8)	= 3	= 13
	= 4	= 14
	= 5	= 15
	= 6	= 16
	= 7*	= 17
	= 8*	= 18
	= 9*	= 19
	= 10	= 20

Two sample problems are done for you.

*More difficult problems.

Brainteaser X

If you know why there are "special numbers," write your answers next to the number in the space provided.

a. 93,000,000 _____   g. 5280 _____

b. 2 _____   h. 7 _____

c. 13 _____   i. 240,000 _____

d. 186,000 _____   j. 2000 _____

e. 22.7 _____   k. 52 _____

f. 6 _____   l. 1776 _____

How many more "special numbers" can you think of?

Brainteaser XI

This brainteaser will test your ability to diverge your thought process. Good luck!

If you cross out eleven letters, you will have exciting math.

EFIXVCIETLIENTGTEMRASTH

Name _____

The Choice Is Yours

SKILLS: Measurement
Inequalities

Materials: 5″ x 8″ cards numbered 1 through 6 (4 cards of each number for a total of 24 cards)

Object: To win, the player must be correct in guessing as to whether the eighth card (the last card in line) is greater than or less than the preceding card.

How to Play: Shuffle all 24 cards and place 8 of them, unexposed, on the ledge of the chalkboard. Align the cards so that everyone sees only the backs of the cards.

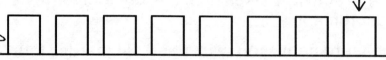

This activity is the teacher opposing the class. Choose a class member to speak for the students. Instruct the student that when he makes decisions, these decisions will be based on the following numbers: 1 2 3 4 5 6.

These are to be written on the chalkboard.

Now, show the very next card to everyone in the classroom.

Teacher: Before we look at the first card on the ledge, we have all seen the very next card (suppose it is a 2). You are the player who will represent the class, and you must decide as to whether the first card on the ledge will be greater than 2 or less than 2. Remember that your choices are on the chalkboard. They are 1, 2, 3, 4, 5 or 6. If you make the correct choice, you may continue guessing down the line. Your goal is to try to reach the eighth and final card. If you are incorrect, it will then be my turn. I may also continue guessing down the line as long as my guesses are correct. A wrong answer on my part will give the turn back to you.

looks like a fun game!

GA1094

The student now looks at the 2 and might say, "I think the card (at the chalkboard) is greater than 2." And now perhaps when the teacher exposes this first card on the ledge, it turns out to be a 5. The student was correct in his coice. The teacher will place the 5 over the 2 so that all eyes will now concentrate on this 5.

At this time the player must base his decision on the 5. Perhaps the player at this point says, "I think that the next card will be less than 5." Suppose the next card on the ledge is a 5. The player would then be incorrect, and it will now be the teacher's turn to guess at the next unexposed card on the chalkboard ledge.

Play may go back and forth this way until the eighth or last card is reached. A correct answer at this point will decide the winner of the game. An incorrect answer at this point will make a winner out of the other team.

The format of this activity makes an excellent tool for reviewing concepts involving measurement.

For linear measurement, you will need 24 cards, four of each card described below.

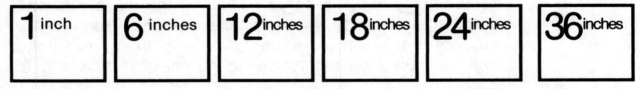

When using these cards, remember to write the choices on the chalkboard.

In this instance:

    1 inch   6 inches   12 inches   18 inches   24 inches   36 inches

You may also want to test the classes' knowledge of money.

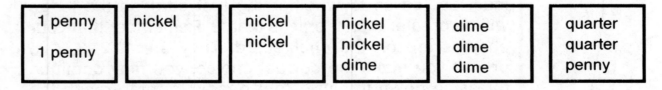

The distribution remains four of each card.

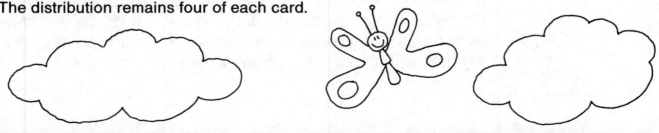

GA1094

Equivalent Fractions

SKILLS: Equivalent Fractions
Improper Fractions
Mixed Numbers

The following gameboards can be constructed using one-inch graph paper. This will enable you to work with thirds, fourths, and fifths.

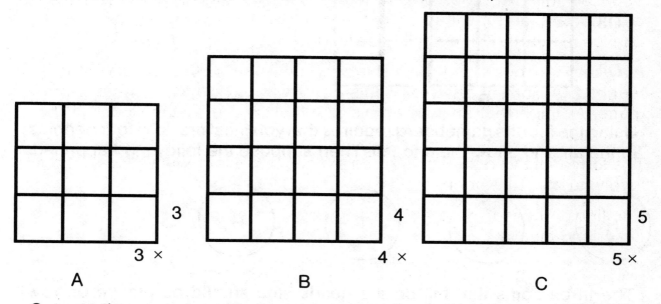

Cut out the squares with the above dimensions and paste them onto oaktag or poster board. In addition to the squares, you will need coins, preferably pennies. If coins are not available, any kind of flat circular objects that easily display heads or tails will suffice.

For gameboard A, you will need 9 pennies, gameboard B will require 16 pennies and gameboard C will require 25 pennies.

The object of the activity is to toss pennies into the air, allow them to fall on a flat surface area and place only those that land heads on the top row of the gameboard. If you are using the gameboard for thirds, each player will have 3 tries to toss 3 pennies on each try. Only those pennies that come up heads are to be placed on the thirds gameboard and on the correct row. Toss one, use row one; toss two, use row two and so on.

Got a penny?
I need one
more penny for
gameboard C.

GA1094

Follow this sample play on a fourths gameboard:

Row   fourths

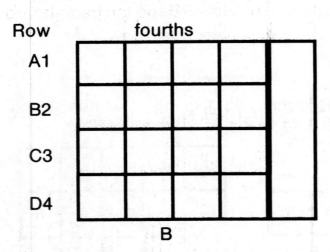

A1

B2

C3

D4

      B

Using the fourths gameboard requires that you must first toss four pennies in the air and allow them to fall. Then suppose the following happened:

The three coins that fell on the heads side should be placed on row A1 in the following way:

Row

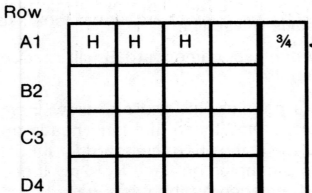

A1 | H | H | H | | ¾ | ←recorded as

B2

C3

D4

The player would then toss four pennies and suppose this time the coins fell this way:

The coins that fell heads should be placed on Row B2 and the gameboard would look like this:

Row

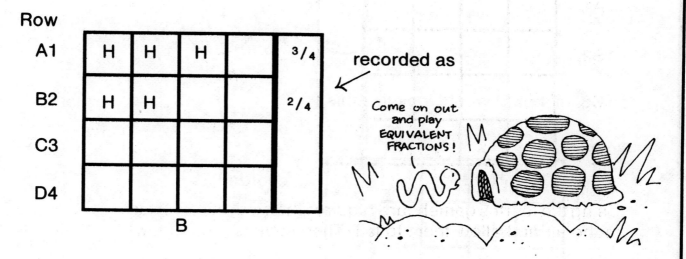

Row					
A1	H	H	H		3/4
B2	H	H			2/4
C3					
D4					

B

recorded as

Come on out and play EQUIVALENT FRACTIONS!

Once again the same player would toss four pennies onto the flat surface area. Suppose the four coins fell thusly:

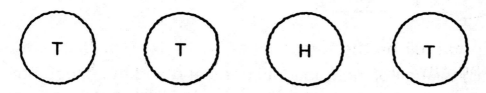

After placing the one head on line C3, the gameboard would look like this:

Row

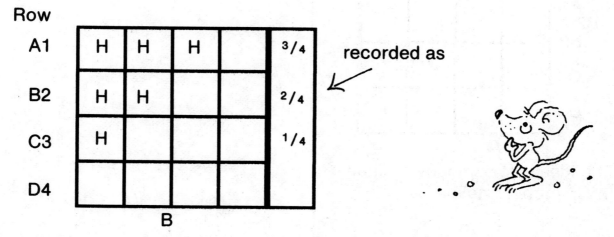

Row					
A1	H	H	H		3/4
B2	H	H			2/4
C3	H				1/4
D4					

B

recorded as

The player would take one more turn tossing four pennies.

GA1094

Perhaps the coins fell this way:

The gameboard would look like this:

Row

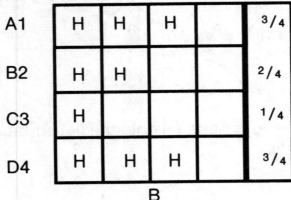

Row					
A1	H	H	H		3/4
B2	H	H			2/4
C3	H				1/4
D4	H	H	H		3/4

B

recorded as

The player should take all of the fractional parts and add them together. This is done by moving the pennies from Row D4 to fill in the missing spaces on Rows A1 and B2.

By adding the fractions, the player can see that:

A1 = 3/4

B2 = 2/4

C3 = 1/4

D4 = 3/4
——————
9/4

The idea is to somehow reduce the improper fraction 9/4.

54

GA1094

Row

A1	H	H	H	↗
B2	H	H	↗	
C3	H			
D4	H	H	H	

B

So, if you move the three coins from D4 to the empty spaces on A1 and B2, then . . .

What a great way to learn fractions!

the final gameboard should look like this:

Row

A1	H	H	H	H
B2	H	H	H	H
C3	H			
D4				

$4/4 = 1$

$4/4 = 1$

$1/4 = 1/4$

$9/4 = 2\ 1/4$

$9/4 = 2$ complete lines of coins and $1/4$ of the next line.

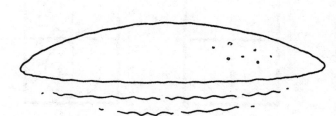

GA1094

Stoplights

SKILLS: Base Three
       Place Value
       Basic Addition Facts

The following designs are representative symbols of traffic lights. Each symbol represents a particular number. Also, each circle within the traffic light is divided into two parts. Each part is a candidate for shading.

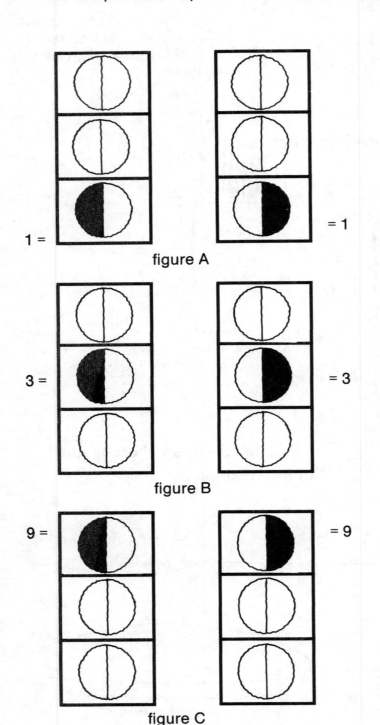

figure A

figure B

figure C

The number 1 can be created by shading either side of the bottom light (figure A).

The number 3 is created by shading either side of the middle light (figure B).

The number 9 is created by shading either side of the top light (figure C).

GA1094

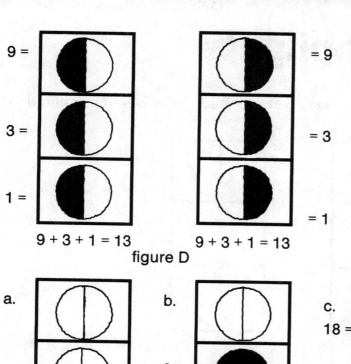

9 =
3 =
1 =

9 + 3 + 1 = 13

= 9
= 3
= 1

9 + 3 + 1 = 13

figure D

The number 13 is created by shading either side of all three circles (figure D).

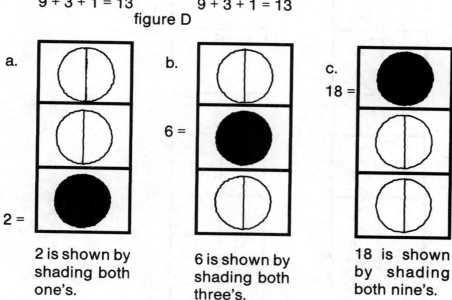

a.

2 =

2 is shown by shading both one's.

b.

6 =

6 is shown by shading both three's.

c.

18 =

18 is shown by shading both nine's.

Using the above information, two more examples:

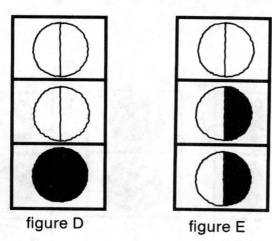

figure D

figure E

Figure D is created to show the sum of 2 and figure E shows the sum of 4.

57

GA1094

Stoplights

Can you solve these problems by shading the correct parts of each traffic light?

a.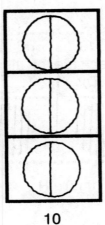

10

b.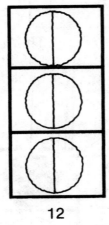

12

c.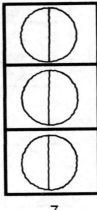

7

d.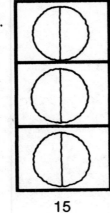

15

e.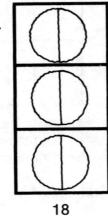

18

f.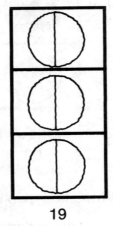

19

Can you solve the problems below?

g.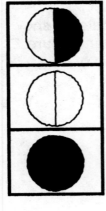

h.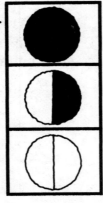

i.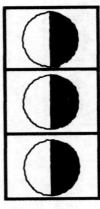

j.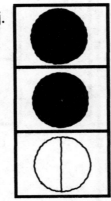

k.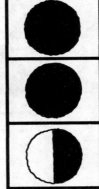

If you are ready to work with numbers greater than 26, you will need to know the following: numbers greater than 26 require two traffic lights working together.

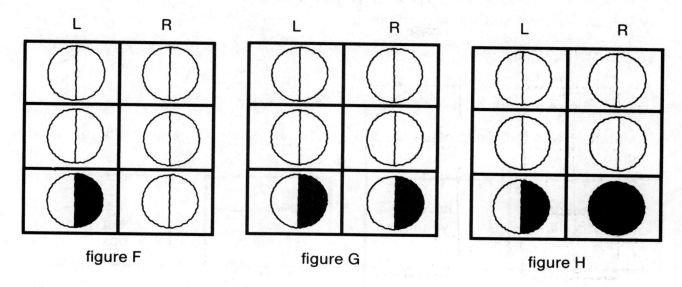

L   R   L   R   L   R

figure F   figure G   figure H

The left side indicates numbers greater than 26; the right side indicates numbers less than and includes 26.

figure F = 27

figure G = 28

figure H = 29

GA1094

Bulls and Bears

SKILLS: Positive and Negative Integers
Fractions
Decimals
Money

For 2, 3 or 4 players

Materials Needed: Four cards (5″ x 8″) with the name of one company on each card.

Consolidated Electronics	Universal Dynamics	Federated Toys Unlimited	Acme Sweet Shops

Playing cards that indicate stock movement.
Playing cards should be 3″ x 5″.
Black cards indicate *up* or *positive* movement.
Red cards indicate *down* or *negative* movement.

Distribution for Black Cards

Face Value of Card:	1/8	1/4	3/8	1/2	5/8	3/4	7/8	1	2	3	
Deck Distribution of Card:	6	4	4	3	2	2	1	2	1	1	= 26 cards

Distribution for Red Cards

Face Value of Card:	1/8	1/4	3/8	1/2	5/8	3/4	7/8	1	2	3	
Deck Distribution of Card:	4	2	1	1	1	1	1	1	1	1	= 14 cards

Object: To control the company with the greatest stock market value.

How to Play: All four companies represent brand-new companies, each offering public stock for the first time. The first-time offering is called an "Initial Public Offering." The issue price of each company's stock will be $20. Therefore stock market trading will begin at $20 per share.

Trading may be explained in the following way: each company's stock will either advance or decline according to dollar units (in this case, the black or red playing cards). If a stock advances 2 points (black card), it is then understood that this stock is now trading at 22 or 22 dollars per share. Perhaps the next playing card is red (negative movement); then the value of this 22 dollar stock would be lower. Perhaps the red card indicated 3 points; then this particular stock of 22 dollars would now be valued at 19 dollars per share.

Stocks may also trade in parts of units. This kind of trade unit is divided into eighths.

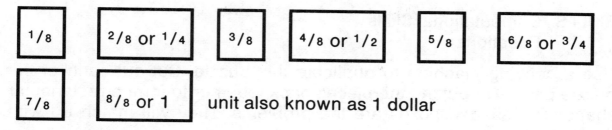

| 1/8 | 2/8 or 1/4 | 3/8 | 4/8 or 1/2 | 5/8 | 6/8 or 3/4 |

| 7/8 | 8/8 or 1 | unit also known as 1 dollar

A trade of 1/8 equates to $0.125
           1/4 equates to $0.25
           3/8 equates to $0.375
           1/2 equates to $0.50
           5/8 equates to $0.625
           3/4 equates to $0.75
           7/8 equates to $0.875
           8/8 equates to $1.00

and one quarter equates to one pack of gum!

The red and black playing cards should be shuffled together, forming one deck of forty cards.

Each player will choose one of the four companies whose stock will now be offered for trade.

How to Play: Each player will take a turn at tossing two number cubes (each cube has six faces and is numbered 1 through 6). The numbers on the top face of each cube are then added together. This sum indicates to the player the card that he/she is due from the playing card deck.

Example:

5 + 3 = 8

When counting to the eighth card in the deck, perhaps this card is a black card (positive movement) and on the face of the card is 3/4; then the stock in the player's company will advance 3/4 or 75 cents per share.

All players will take turns in tossing the number cubes and then use this particular sum to locate the card from the playing card deck.

The winner will be the first player to hold stock in a company with a per share value of $32.

GA1094

Puzzle Parts

SKILLS: Computational Skills
   Equations

Name_____

Use a copying machine to duplicate this puzzle. Cut out each of the puzzle parts. Try putting the pieces back together to form a rectangular shape. The shaded boxes are the problems. They will match up with the correct answers.

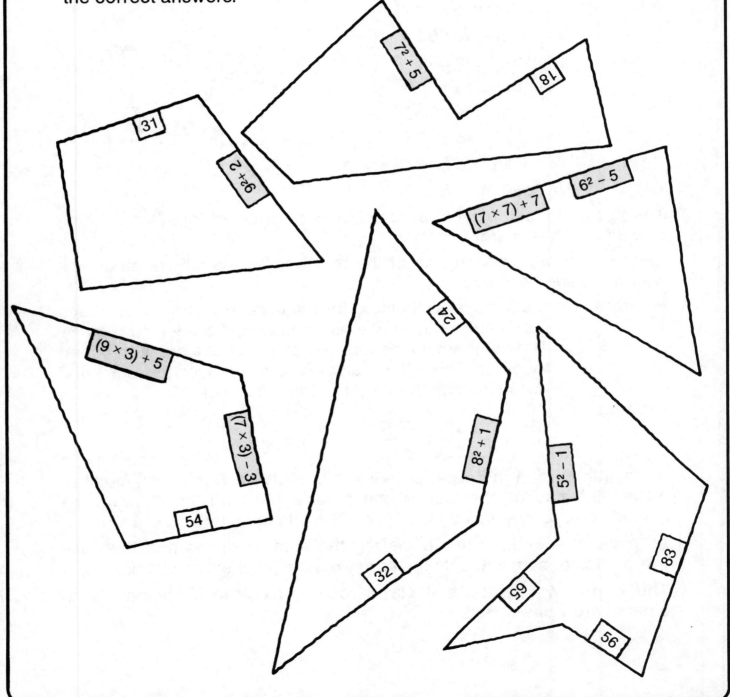

Use a copying machine to duplicate this puzzle. Cut out each of the puzzle parts. Try putting the pieces back together to form a tropical bird. The shaded boxes are the problems. They will match up with the correct answers.

63

GA1094

Recreational and Exciting Multiplication

A most interesting approach, Comrade.

SKILLS: Multiplication Facts
         Powers of 2

Some interesting ways of approaching multiplication.

The Russian Peasant

The problem is 20×30. Write one factor under Column A and the other factor under Column B.

A	B
20	30

Step 1:   The procedure is to always take half of the factors in Column A and at the same time, always double the factors under Column B.

A	B
20	30
10	60
5	120
2½	240

Step 2:   In Column A, when you get to a number with a half such as 2½, just drop the half and record the whole number. Continue this process until you reach 1 in Column A.

A	B
20	30
10	60
5	120
2	240
1	480

Step 3:   Once you have reached 1 in Column A, concentrate now with the numbers in this column (A). If any number in Column A is even, then the entire row (horizontal) is to be crossed out and eliminated.

GA1094

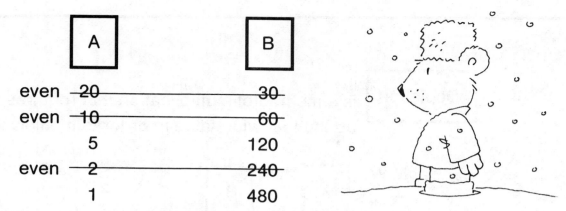

	A		B
even	~~20~~		~~30~~
even	~~10~~		~~60~~
	5		120
even	~~2~~		~~240~~
	1		480

Step 4:   The answer to the original problem 20 × 30 lies with the remaining partial products in Column B.

$$\begin{array}{r} 120 \\ + 480 \\ \hline 600 \end{array} = 20 \times 30$$

Another example:
    24 × 32

   *Remember, one half of Column A, double Column B. If you come to a number with a half, drop the half. Continue this process until you have a 1 in Column A.

A	B
24	32
12	64
6	128
3	256
1	512

   *Remember to cross out the entire row if any number in Column A is even.

A	B	
~~24~~	~~32~~	
~~12~~	~~64~~	
~~6~~	~~128~~	
3	256	answer 256
1	512	$\begin{array}{r} +512 \\ \hline 768 \end{array} = 24 \times 32$

Try this method with a. 14 × 40, b. 22 × 34, c. 18 × 35.

GA1094

| Depletion | is a method of multiplication that requires setting up the following table in order to multiply 20 × 30. |

Table W

A	B
1 × 30 =	30
2 × 30 =	60
4 × 30 =	120
8 × 30 =	240
16 × 30 =	480

If you look for a pattern, you should see that the factors in Column A are doubling as well as the products in Column B, which are also doubling.

In order to multiply 20 × 30, use Table W to search out the answer.

$$20 × 30$$

In Table W you can see
16 × 30 = 480
4 × 30 = 120

if you add   16   and   480
              + 4   + 120
             20 × 30   =   600

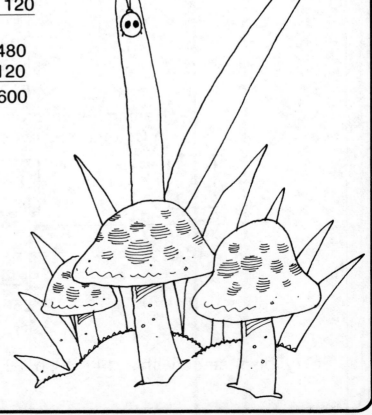

Another example: 24 × 32

Table X

A	B
1 × 32 =	32
2 × 32 =	64
4 × 32 =	128
8 × 32 =	256
16 × 32 =	512

GA1094

The problem: 24 × 32 using Table X.

$$16 \times 32 = 512$$
$$+ \underline{8 \times 32} = \underline{256}$$
$$24 \times 32 = 768$$

...Again using Table X,
we can multiply
30 × 32...

Again using Table X, we can multiply 30 × 32.

$$16 \times 32 = 512$$
$$8 \times 32 = 256$$
$$4 \times 32 = 128$$
$$+ \underline{2 \times 32} = + \underline{64}$$
$$30 \times 32 = 960$$

By adding one more step to Table X, you could multiply 35 × 32.

Table X

A	B
1 × 32 =	32
2 × 32 =	64
4 × 32 =	128
8 × 32 =	256
16 × 32 =	512
32 × 32 =	1024

35 × 32

$$32 \times 32 = 1024$$
$$2 \times 32 = 64$$
$$+ \underline{1 \times 32} = \underline{32}$$
$$35 \times 32 = 1120$$

Use the depletion method with

a. 14 × 40   b. 18 × 25   c. 24 × 25   d. 37 × 25

GA1094

We can use a blank 10 × 10 square to multiply two factors.

To multiply 20 × 30, you would write 30 on the chart 20 times and then total each column.

30	30								
30	30								
30	30								
30	30								
30	30								
30	30								
30	30								
30	30								
30	30								
30	30								

300 + 300

$20 \times 30 = 300 + 300 = 600$

Another example: 32 × 27

27	27	27	27						
27	27	27	27						
27	27	27							
27	27	27							
27	27	27							
27	27	27							
27	27	27							
27	27	27							
27	27	27							
27	27	27							

270 + 270 + 270 + 54

```
  270
  270
  270
+  54
```

= $32 \times 27 = 864$

GA1094

Crosshatch Multiplication

Shaded rectangle is equal to a ten.

Line is equal to a one.

To multiply 21 × 32, one factor (21) will be drawn horizontally and the other factor (32) will be drawn over the first factor in a vertical position.

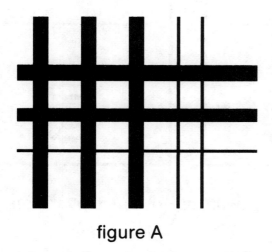

figure A

The answer lies in knowing the following:

1. Where shaded rectangle crosses shaded rectangle, it makes a hundred.

2. Where shaded rectangle crosses line it makes a ten.

3. Where line crosses line, it makes a one.

In figure A, 1. shaded rectangle crosses a shaded rectangle six times.

$$6 \times 100 = 600$$

2. Shaded rectangle crosses a line 7 times.

$$7 \times 10 = 70$$

3. Line crosses line 2 times.

$$2 \times 1 = \underline{2}$$

$$21 \times 32 = 672$$

GA1094

Sub-Add

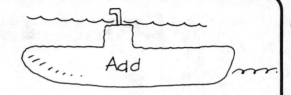

SKILLS: Basic Facts Addition
            Basic Facts Subtraction

Materials: cards 2½″ × 3½″ numbered   1 to 10 (6 of each card)
                                    11 to 14 (3 of each card)

Cards should look something like these:

The game is for two players or two teams with up to four players on each team.

Object: To have the fewest or no cards remaining after all cards from the unexposed pile are used.

        The game is automatically over if a team uses up all of the ten exposed cards.

How to Play: 1. Each player or team is dealt ten cards faceup. All of the unused cards are placed in a pile facedown.

                2. In turn, Player A exposes the top card from the facedown deck.

                3. The number on this card indicates to Player A the number to be reached by adding or subtracting as many of the ten faceup cards in front of the team.

GA1094

Wish I
could
play.

4. An ideal situation would be for Player A to be able to use all ten of the exposed face cards in which case Player A would have an automatic win.

5. Follow this sample play. Suppose the ten faceup cards for Player A were

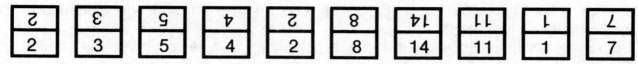

| 2 | 3 | 5 | 4 | 2 | 8 | 14 | 11 | 1 | 7 |

and perhaps the card from the unexposed pile was a $\boxed{6\,/\,9}$ Player A wants to use as many of the ten cards as possible.

$$\boxed{14} - \boxed{11} = 3 + \boxed{3} + \boxed{2} + \boxed{1} = 9$$

| 2 | 3 | 5 | 4 | 2 | 8 | 14 | 11 | 1 | 7 |
| | × | | | × | | × | × | × | |

$$\boxed{5} + \boxed{4} = 9, \quad \boxed{7} + \boxed{2} = 9$$

| 2 | 3 | 5 | 4 | 2 | 8 | 14 | 11 | 1 | 7 |
| × | × | × | × | × | | × | × | × | × |

After a round of play, Player A has one card left $\boxed{8}$. Play now goes to Player B.

Perhaps during A's second turn, the card from the unused deck is a $\boxed{10}$. A's only card left is an $\boxed{8}$ and cannot make a 10; therefore A must take the 10 into his area and await another turn.

Perhaps on the next turn, A's top card from the unexposed deck is $\boxed{2}$. Then A is able to create $\boxed{10} - \boxed{8} = 2$. When all the exposed cards are gone, play is automatically over and Player A is the winner.

GA1094

Placement Mats

SKILLS: Basic Primary Computational Skills—Addition, Subtraction, Multiplication, Division

For the Round Robin activity, the following gameboards should be constructed on white poster board (22″ × 28″). There are five different gameboards, one for addition, one for subtraction, one for multiplication, one for division, and one gameboard that contains all four operations.

Teams are assigned to each of the five gameboards. A team player will shuffle the 24 answer cards that are assigned to that gameboard. The player is to count out eight answer cards for his team. Players are not to look at their cards until the teacher says, "Go!" At this point, the team will have 45 seconds to match the answer card with the correct question on their assigned gameboard.

Example:

15
15

to match

8 + 7

Each team will be given 30 seconds to check problems and answers. Two points are given for each correct placement.

On the teacher's cue, all of the answer cards should be reshuffled and on the command "Go," the teams will move to the next board in the Round Robin format. Play ends when each team has had an opportunity at each gameboard. The team with the highest point total for all five gameboards is declared the winner.

9 + 5	11 + 7	7 + 7	12 + 6	5 + 13	10 + 5
13 + 2	7 + 9	16 + 2	14 + 4	12 + 0	6 + 7
11 + 5	9 + 9	8 + 9	6 + 8	5 + 7	12 + 3
10 + 6	15 + 1	10 + 0	13 + 4	9 + 3	7 + 10

18 − 5	14 − 9	17 − 5	11 − 8	16 − 8	13 − 5
10 − 5	16 − 0	12 − 2	16 − 3	12 − 8	17 − 0
18 − 2	11 − 5	14 − 1	17 − 2	18 − 6	10 − 6
17 − 4	14 − 7	12 − 5	14 − 3	10 − 10	14 − 0

3 × 6	5 × 5	9 × 0	5 × 3	1 × 10	2 × 8
5 × 2	12 × 2	4 × 5	0 × 9	3 × 8	6 × 4
4 × 3	2 × 10	8 × 2	2 × 7	1 × 11	4 × 4
3 × 5	9 × 2	1 × 8	0 × 8	10 × 0	7 × 3

10 ÷ 2	12 ÷ 3	15 ÷ 5	20 ÷ 5	12 ÷ 2	10 ÷ 1
16 ÷ 8	10 ÷ 5	9 ÷ 9	14 ÷ 2	18 ÷ 6	18 ÷ 9
9 ÷ 3	14 ÷ 7	21 ÷ 7	18 ÷ 3	21 ÷ 3	20 ÷ 4
12 ÷ 6	20 ÷ 2	15 ÷ 3	10 ÷ 10	18 ÷ 2	12 ÷ 4

13 + 3	8 + 5	4 × 3	16 − 9	16 ÷ 8	5 + 11
0 × 12	12 × 2	9 + 7	11 + 7	20 ÷ 4	17 − 5
20 ÷ 1	14 − 5	11 − 10	17 − 8	1 + 12	3 × 7
12 − 3	9 + 7	18 ÷ 6	2 × 9	18 ÷ 2	17 − 10

Each gameboard contains 24 problems and should be accompanied with 24 answer cards (2½″ × 3½″). There should be an answer card for every problem on the gameboard. This Round Robin is for five players or five teams with two players on each team.

GA1094

Bunches and Bunches of Multiples

Rah! Rah! — Multiples!

SKILLS: Multiplication
         Multiples
         Common Multiples

When you are working with multiples, it might be easier and more understandable for you if you think of multiples as "making bunches of."

Example:

Bunches of 4

4	8	12	16	20	24	28	32	36

Bunches of 3

3	6	9	12	15	18	21	24	27

Examining both lines of multiples, you can see that some multiples appear on both lines.

12   and   24   are the multiples that appear on both lines. They are known as common multiples.   12   is the lowest common multiple for 3 and 4.

Finish both lines of multiples.

Multiples of 2

2	4		8					

Multiples of 3

3	6			15				

What are the common multiples of 2 and 3?

☐ ☐ ☐

What is the lowest common multiple of 2 and 3?

☐

Finish these lines of multiples.

Multiples of 6

6								

Multiples of 8

8								

Multiples of 10

10								

GA1094

More on Lowest Common Multiple or L.C.M.

SKILLS: Multiples   Lowest Common Multiples
Multiplication   Prime Factors

Another way of finding the lowest common multiple of numbers is to deal with prime numbers or, in this instance, the prime factors of the numbers.

Some of the more important prime factors to remember are 2, 3, 5, 7, 11.

Follow this procedure to find the L.C.M. for 6 and 8.

1. Set up this chart.

$$6 \quad | \quad 8$$

2. Factor both numbers to their prime factors (those factors listed above).

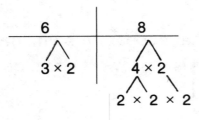

3. Check the factors on both sides of this chart to see if any of the prime factors are repeated. If so, cross them out on the lesser side.

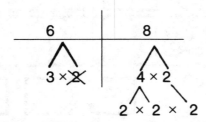

The remaining factors when multiplied will indicate the L.C.M. In this instance, the L.C.M. for 6 and 8 is 3 × 2 × 2 × 2 or 24.

Find the lowest common multiple for the following:

a.   9   12

b.   6   12

c.   14   30

d.   The super one*

   6   8   10

Loskor

SKILLS: Basic Skills—Addition, Subtraction, Multiplication, Division

Materials: The large gameboard containing two parts—A and B. Each part contains numerals 25 to 2, two sets of regular dice, 24 Bingo chips per team.

Object: The winner is the team with the lowest score at the game's end.

How to Play: 1. The game may be played with one player on each gameboard or two teams with up to four players on a team.

Wanna play Loskor?

2. In turn, each team tosses the two sets of dice. Example: 6, 3, 2, 5

3. The team must use all dice to form any operation or combinations of operations (+, −, ×, ÷).

The idea is to see on how many numbered cells you can place a Bingo chip. Remember, you must use the four dice.

Example: a. $(6 \times 5) - (3 + 2) =$ $\boxed{25}$

b. $\dfrac{[(5 \times 2) \times 3]}{6} =$ $\boxed{5}$

c. $(3 + 2 + 6) - 5 =$ $\boxed{6}$

This team would be able to cover 25, 5 and 6.

4. Each team will have two minutes per round.

5. After each team has four turns, all of the uncovered numbers are added up and *held against you!*

6. The team with the lowest score wins!

GA1094

Gameboard
B

2	3	4
5	6	7
8	9	10
11	12	13

14	15	16
17	18	19
20	21	22
23	24	25

Gameboard
B

Loskor

25	24	23
22	21	20
19	18	17
16	15	14

Gameboard
A

13	12	11
10	9	8
7	6	5
4	3	2

GA1094

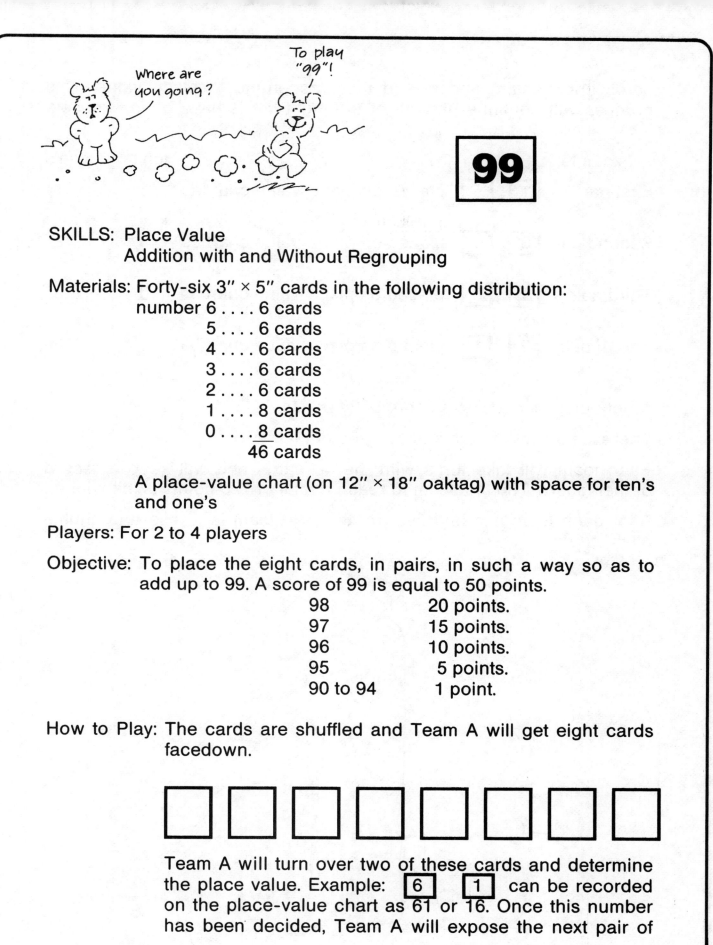

Where are you going?

To play "99"!

99

SKILLS: Place Value
Addition with and Without Regrouping

Materials: Forty-six 3″ × 5″ cards in the following distribution:

number 6 . . . . 6 cards
5 . . . . 6 cards
4 . . . . 6 cards
3 . . . . 6 cards
2 . . . . 6 cards
1 . . . . 8 cards
0 . . . . 8 cards
46 cards

A place-value chart (on 12″ × 18″ oaktag) with space for ten's and one's

Players: For 2 to 4 players

Objective: To place the eight cards, in pairs, in such a way so as to add up to 99. A score of 99 is equal to 50 points.

98	20 points.
97	15 points.
96	10 points.
95	5 points.
90 to 94	1 point.

How to Play: The cards are shuffled and Team A will get eight cards facedown.

☐ ☐ ☐ ☐ ☐ ☐ ☐ ☐

Team A will turn over two of these cards and determine the place value. Example: 6 1 can be recorded on the place-value chart as 61 or 16. Once this number has been decided, Team A will expose the next pair of

77

cards and declare and record them according to place value. This process will continue until all of the eight cards have been exposed.

			ten's	one's
Example:				
First pair	1 5	placed on place-value chart as	5	1
Second pair	3 2	placed on place-value chart as	3	2
Third pair	3 0	placed on place-value chart as	0	3
Fourth pair	2 1	placed on place-value chart as	1	2
			9	8

Ninety-eight is equal to a score of 20 points.

There is no score for an answer greater than 99.

Each team will take turns with the 46 cards and will keep a record of their score. The first team to reach a total of 125 points is the winner.

After each team has had its turn, the next team is to use and shuffle all 46 cards.

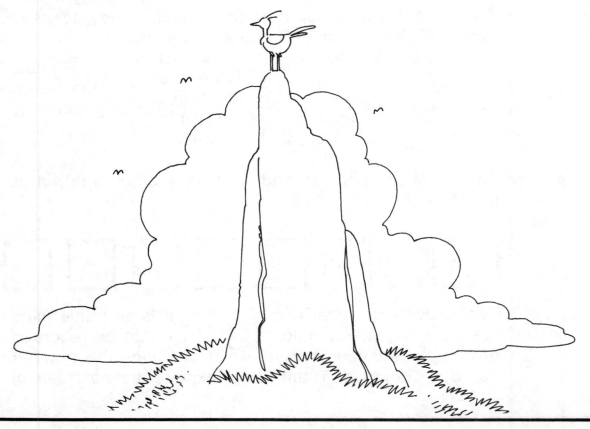

GA1094

Aha! Very Interesting

SKILLS: Patterning
Multiplication
Addition

Working with patterns can be most interesting, especially when you are able to arrive at a solution to the problem.

Consider the series below. It is a series of consecutive numbers. The problem as presented is to find the sum of the numbers involved. Even further, the problem is to find the sum of any series of consecutive numbers.

Example:

15, 16, 17, 18, 19, 20, 21, 22, 23, 24, 25

An important problem-solving technique is to be able to take any difficult problem and make it simpler.

Each series below has three numbers and the answer.

$$3, 4, 5 = 12$$

$$8, 9, 10 = 27$$

Through careful examination, you can see that the sum of the series is three times the middle number.

$$6, 7, 8 = 21$$

Another series:

$$4, 5, 6, 7, 8 = 30$$

$$13, 14, 15, 16, 17 = 75$$

Examine the pattern between the middle number of the series and the answer.

GA1094

At this point you should be able to appreciate the formula that will allow you to accurately predict the answer to any series of consecutive numbers as long as the amount of numbers in the series is odd.

The formula: the middle series × the amount of numbers in the series

17, 18, 19, 20, 21, 22, 23,   20 × 7 = 140

Find the sum in each series of numbers.

a. 26, 27, 28, 29, 30, 31, 32, 33, 34

b. 6, 7, 8, 9, 10, 11, 12, 13, 14, 15, 16

c. 56, 57, 58, 59, 60

d. 60, 61, 62, 63, 64, 65, 66, 67, 68

Some perceptive observers will probably discover another approach to solving the series above. Consider this:

4, 5, 6, 7, 8

We have 4 + 8 = 12
5 + 7 = 12
24
6 middle number
30

GA1094

Another example:

55, 56, 57, 58, 59, 60, 61

$$55 + 61 = 116$$
$$56 + 60 = 116$$
$$57 + 59 = 116$$
$$\underline{}$$
$$348$$
$$\underline{58} \text{ middle}$$
$$406 \text{ number}$$

Although this is a very interesting approach, it would be a very burdensome one if there were 97 numbers in the series.

Now comes another interesting question regarding the original question. What happens if the series of consecutive numbers is an even amount and not an odd amount?

17, 18, 19, 20, 21, 22, 23, 24

Can you come up with a formula for this problem?
Remember that problem-solving technique of making a difficult problem simpler and then looking for the solution?

2, 3, 4, 5
8, 9, 10, 11

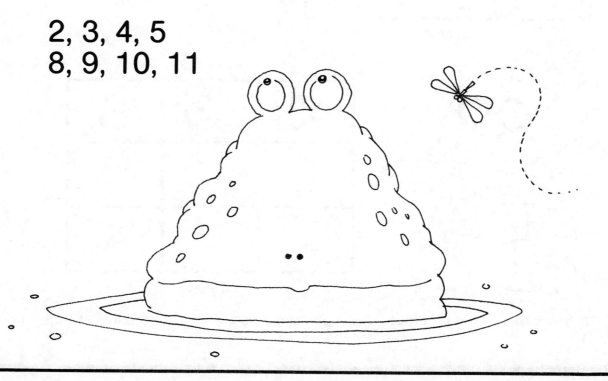

GA1094

4, 5, 6

SKILLS: Number Patterns
       Whole Numbers
       Fractions

This activity encourages the use of thinking skills that are necessary to pattern searches. There is one mystery pattern contained in each box. Each box is made up of nine cells. The cells are noted alphabetically. Each box also contains three known cells.

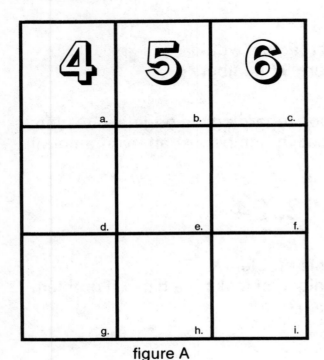

figure A

The idea is to look for a pattern in figure A and then complete the empty cells in the pattern box with a series of numbers. The order of the cells to be completed should follow alphabetical order.

Figure A would be completed by writing the series of numbers shown in figure B.

4 a.	5 b.	6 c.
7 d.	8 e.	9 f.
10 g.	11 h.	12 i.

figure B

In this example, each empty cell was completed with a difference of plus one or D = 1.

GA1094

If you correctly solve the next example (figure C), you can determine that the empty cells are also completed with a difference of plus one or D = 1.

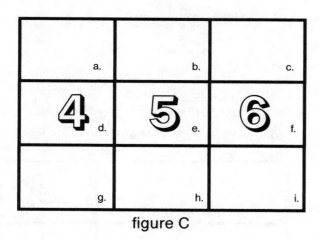

figure C

Figure D represents the solution to figure C.

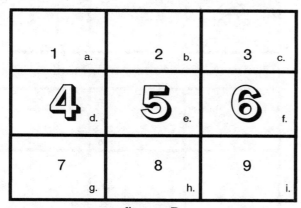

figure D

The difference in the solution box is plus one or D = 1.

Follow this same format and solve the box of figure E, by finding the difference or the value for D.

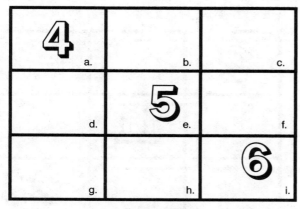

figure E

Solve the following solution boxes by determining the value for D. Remember that all of the empty cells in each solution box should follow the alphabetical sequence described in the examples of figures A, B, C and D.

AA.

a.	b. 4	c.
d.	e. 5	f.
g.	h. 6	i.

BB.

a.	b.	c. 4
d.	e. 5	f.
g. 6	h.	i.

CC.

a.	b.	c. 4
d.	e.	f. 5
g.	h.	i. 6

DD.

a.	b.	c.
d.	e.	f.
g. 4	h. 5	i. 6

EE.

a. 1	b.	c.
d.	e. 25	f.
g.	h.	i. 81

FF.

a. 2	b.	c.
d.	e. 11	f.
g.	h.	i. 23

GA1094

The Thirteen C's

SKILLS: Estimation
               Subtraction, Addition

This activity deals with your ability to estimate as well as your knowledge about the thirteen original United States colonies. The colonies are listed below. Some of them are abbreviated so as to make this activity somewhat more challenging.

1. North Carolina

2. SC

3. Georgia

4. NY

5. New Hampshire

6. NJ

7. DE

8. CT

9. PA

10. Rhode Island

11. VA

12. MD

13. Massachusetts

GA1094

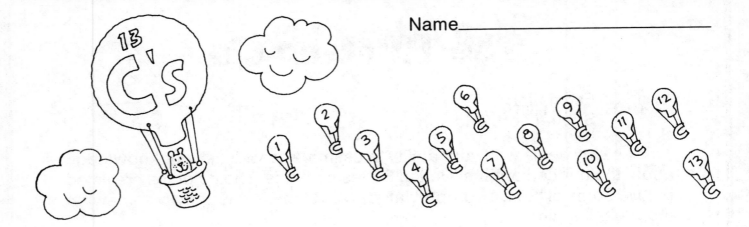

Rules:

Before you attempt to answer the questions, make a guess and record it under the column headed "Guess." Do this for all three questions. Next to the "Guess" column is the column headed "Actual Answer." In this column, solve the problem as stated in the question and record the correct answer. The difference between your guess and the correct answer should be recorded in the column headed "Difference."

After recording the three answers, total the three differences and compare your total answer with some classmates. The lowest number in the difference column (total) will indicate the winner.

The Questions:

1. How many letters are in the names of the thirteen original colonies?

2. How many vowels are in the names of the thirteen original colonies?

3. How many syllables are in the names of the thirteen original colonies?

Remember, record your guess first!

	Guess	Actual Answer	Difference
1.			
2.			
3.			
		Total of Differences	

GA1094

Answer Key

Understanding a Million   page 1

1 million inches equals approximately 17.05 miles.

1 million seconds is approximately 11.5 days.

For a Million, Your Cost Would Be . . .
                                              page 2

a. $750,000   f. $1,490,000
b. $900,000   g. $1,010,000
c. $1,250,000   h. $1,050,000
d. $1,650,000   i. $7,250,000
e. $1,000,000   j. $1,290,000

A Million Dollars Could Buy . . . page 4

1. 50 automobiles
2. 25 boats
3. 8 houses
4. 2 ranches
5. 3 airplanes
6. 20 horses
7. 10,000 skateboards
8. 2857 VCRs
9. 1000 video cam-corders
10. 28 charities

Split Second Addition Fill-Ins   page 8

K	L	M	N	O
245	624	613	632	309
641	327	811	236	606
344	129	415	137	804
542	822	514	533	507
146	525	217	335	903

P	Q	R	S	T
405	127	541	733	314
306	325	640	436	215
207	424	244	535	611
702	820	343	139	512
504	523	145	238	710

Patchwork Quilt   page 11

1. Column A 34
2. Row 4
3. 4 corners = 12
4. Columns D + E = 53
5. Row 3
6. Row 2
7. Column C
8. 137

It would be helpful to know the totals of . . .

Columns	A	B	C	D	E
	34	31	19	28	25

Rows	1	2	3	4	5
	17	39	31	19	31

GA1094

Patch These Quilts   page 13

a.	16	i.	56
b.	17	j.	16
c.	9	k.	245
d.	10	l.	10
e.	27	m.	26
f.	33	n.	20
g.	25	o.	112
h.	140	p.	4

It's All in Black and White   pages 14-16

A. any number in the twenties
B. any even number
C. any factor of 30
D. any square number
E. any prime number
F. any number relating to time and calendar
G. any power of 2
H. any palindromic number
I. any value of U.S. coins
J. any multiple of 15
K. any number with a 7 somewhere in that number
L. your choice

Fraction Action Cards   page 28

a. $10/8 = 1\frac{1}{4}$ g. $9/8 = 1\frac{1}{8}$
b. $4/2 = 2$ h. $4/4 = 1$
c. $11/8 = 1\frac{3}{8}$ i. $7/8$
d. $10/8 = 1\frac{1}{4}$ j. $7/4 = 1\frac{3}{4}$
e. $9/8 = 1\frac{1}{8}$ k. $8/4 = 2$
f. $7/4 = 1\frac{3}{4}$

And the Answer Is . . .   page 30

1.	213	4.	171
	292		204
	420		300
	925		675

2.	192	5.	220
	237		151
	482		413
	911		784

3.	431	6.	140
	205		322
	312		106
	948		568

More of And the Answer Is . . . page 31

7.	8402	10.	5151	13.	3311
	1173		2543		1234
	0102		1002		5021
	9677		8696		9566

8.	1403	11.	1643	14.	5172
	1256		5021		1203
	4210		2311		2414
	6869		8975		8789

9.	2603	12.	1037
	1014		3212
	3281		1640
	6898		5889

GA1094

Mickey Moose
page 34

3 times the number plus 1.

Mickey Moose Problems
page 36

a. 80
b. 70
c. 90
d. 7
e. 15

f. 28
g. 100
h. 20
i. 56
j. 5

Mickey Moose Tables
page 37

a. 5 times the number
pink 5 × 5 = 25
green 5 × 6 = 30
red 5 × 1 = 5

b. 4 times the number
brown 4 × 10 = 40
white 4 × 4 = 16
red 4 × 1 = 4

c. 11 times the number
white 11 × 4 = 44
green 11 × 6 = 66
pink 11 × 5 = 55

d. 7 times the number
yellow 7 × 3 = 21
orange 7 × 7 = 49
brown 7 × 10 = 70

Finding Area
pages 38-39

a. 4 units
b. 2 units
c. 2½ units
d. 3¼ units

i. 2 units
j. 3½ units
k. 2²/₃ units
l. 4 units

Finding Area Units
page 41

a. 3 units
b. 5½ units
c. 4 units

d. 5½ units
e. 5 units
f. 6 units

Geo-Code
page 43

a. 17
b. 14
c. 27

d. 27
e. 52
f. 26

Brainteaser V
page 44

Plan B
1st week: $.64
2nd week: $81.92
3rd week: $10,485.76
4th week: $1,342,177.28

Brainteaser VI
page 45

2 weighings, if you start by placing 3 cubes in each pan.

GA1094

The solution is to cut the 15-inch piece of wood in 3 strategic places.

1 2 3 4 5 6 7 8 9 10 11 12 13 14 15

Cut here 1"

☐1   Piece will be 1 inch.

Cut at 3"
Cut at 7"

☐☐2   Piece will be 2 inches.

☐☐☐☐4

Piece will be 4 inches. Remaining piece will be 8 inches.

Now to be able to count from 1 to 16 using the 4 pieces above:

1. = ☐1

2. = ☐☐2

3. = ☐☐2   ☐1

4. = ☐☐☐☐4

5. = ☐☐☐☐4   ☐1

6. = ☐☐☐☐4   ☐☐2

7. = ☐☐☐☐4   ☐☐2   ☐1

8. = ☐☐☐☐☐☐☐☐8

9. = ☐☐☐☐☐☐☐☐8   ☐1

10. = ☐☐☐☐☐☐☐☐8   ☐☐2

11. = ☐☐☐☐☐☐☐☐8   ☐☐2   ☐1

12. = ☐☐☐☐☐☐☐☐8   ☐☐☐☐4

13. = ☐☐☐☐☐☐☐☐8   ☐☐☐☐4   ☐1

14. = ☐☐☐☐☐☐☐☐8   ☐☐☐☐4   ☐☐2

15. = ☐☐☐☐☐☐☐☐8   ☐☐☐☐4   ☐☐2   ☐1

GA1094

Brainteaser VIII
page 46

Alphabetical order

Brainteaser IX
page 47

1. $(8 + 2) - (9 \times 1) = 1$
   $(9 - 8) + (2 - 1) = 2$
   $(9 - 8) \times (2 + 1) = 3$
   $(9 - 8) + (2 + 1) = 4$
   $[9 - (^8/_2)] \times 1 = 5$
   $(9 + 1) - (8 \div 2) = 6$
   $18 - (9 + 2) = 7$
   $(2 \times 8) - (9 - 1) = 8$
   $28 - 19 = 9$
   $(9 \times 2) - (8 \times 1) = 10$
   $[9 \div (2 + 1)] + 8 = 11$
   $[(8 \div 2) - 1] + 9 = 12$
   $\dfrac{9 + 1}{2} + 8 = 13$

   $(9 + 1) + (8 \div 2) = 14$
   $(9 + 8) - (2 \times 1) = 15$
   $(9 + 8 + 1) - 2 = 16$
   $(9 + 8) \times (2 - 1) = 17$
   $(9 + 8) + (2 - 1) = 18$
   $(9 + 8) + (2 \times 1) = 19$
   $1 + 9 + 2 + 8 = 20$

Brainteaser X
page 48

a. miles earth to sun
b. only even prime number, pair, twin
c. prime number
d. speed of light
e. pi
f. perfect number (factors equal the number $1 + 2 + 3 = 6$)
g. feet in a mile
h. days in a week
i. miles earth to moon
j. pounds in a ton
k. weeks in a year
l. year of the American Revolution

Brainteaser XI
page 48

E P̶I̶X̶ Y C I E̶ T L I E̶ N T̶ G T̶ E M R A S̶ T H

Stoplights
page 58

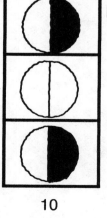

a.

10

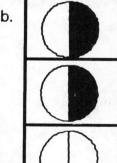

b.

12

c.

7

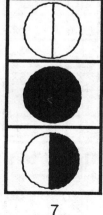

d.

15

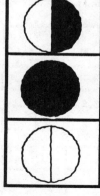

e.

18

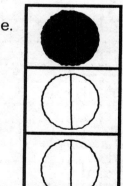

f.

19

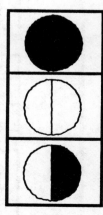

g. = 11   h. = 21   i. = 13   j. = 24   k. = 25

GA1094

More on Lowest Common Mulitple or L.C.M.   page 74

a.
$$\frac{9}{3 \times \cancel{3}} \Big| \frac{12}{3 \times 4}$$
$$2 \times 2$$
$$3 \times 3 \times 2 \times 2 = 36$$

b.
$$\frac{6}{\cancel{2} \times \cancel{3}} \Big| \frac{12}{3 \times 4}$$
$$2 \times 2$$
$$3 \times 2 \times 2 = 12$$

c.
$$\frac{14}{\cancel{2} \times 7} \Big| \frac{30}{5 \times 6}$$
$$2 \times 3$$
$$7 \times 5 \times 2 \times 3 = 210$$

d.
$$\frac{6}{\cancel{2} \times 3} \Big| \frac{8}{\cancel{4 \times 2}} \Big| \frac{10}{2 \times 5}$$
$$\cancel{2} \times 2 \times 2$$
$$3 \times 2 \times 2 \times 2 \times 5 = 120$$

Aha! Very Interesting   page 79

Possible solution to a series with an even amount of numbers: Find the middle pair in the series. Add these numbers together. Multiply this sum by one half of the number of numerals in the series.

6, 7, 8, 9, 10, 11 = middle pair: 8 + 9 = 17

6 numerals in the series divided by ½ equals 3. 17 × 3 = 51

4, 5, 6   pages 83-84

E.

4	4¼	4½
4¾	5	5¼
5½	5¾	6

D = ¼

AA.

3²/₃	4	4¹/₃
4²/₃	5	5¹/₃
5²/₃	6	6¹/₃

D = ¹/₃

BB.

3	3½	4
4½	5	5½
6	6½	7

D = ½

CC.

3¹/₃	3²/₃	4
4¹/₃	4²/₃	5
5¹/₃	5²/₃	6

D = ¹/₃

DD.

–2	–1	0
1	2	3
4	5	6

D = 1

EE.

1	4	9
16	25	36
49	64	81

D = square numbers

FF.

2	3	5
7	11	13
17	19	23

D = prime numbers

The Thirteen C's   page 85

1. Letters 132
2. Vowels 56
3. Syllables 44

GA1094